Novelty KNITS

35 FUN & FABULOUS JUMPER DESIGNS

Gyles and Saethryd Brandreth

Photography by Ingrid Rasmussen

KYLE BOOKS

First published in Great Britain in 2014 by
Kyle Books, an imprint of Kyle Cathie Ltd
192-8 Vauxhall Bridge Road
London SW1V 1DX
general.enquiries@kylebooks.com
www.kylebooks.com

10 9 8 7 6 5 4 3 2 1

ISBN 978 0 85783 264 1

Project Editors: Judith Hannam and Clare Sayer
Editorial Assistant: Claire Rogers
Designer: Isobel Gillan
Photographer: Ingrid Rasmussen
Illustrations: Carol Kearns
Prop Stylist: Polly Webb-Wilson and Catrina Håland
Production: Nic Jones, Gemma John and Lisa Pinnell

A Cataloguing in Publication record for this title is available from the British Library.

Colour reproduction by ALTA London
Printed and bound in China by C&C offset printing Co., Ltd

Contents

Introduction by Gyles Brandreth

Welcome to the Brandreth family knitting book. This is a collection of our favourite knitting patterns for jumpers, chosen by me and by my daughter, Saethryd, and modelled by us and some of our friends. We hope the book will help raise funds for an important charity – Women for Women International – and we hope it will raise a smile, too. It is a book for people who enjoy knitting in general, and colourful, fun knitwear in particular.

The craft of knitting has been part of civilised life for at least a thousand years. The verb 'to knit' comes from the Old English *cnyttan*, to knot. From fragments of material unearthed by archaeologists, we know they were knitting socks in Egypt in the eleventh century. We know, too, they were knitting caps for babies in Spain in the twelfth century. From the fourteenth century, there are several celebrated paintings of the Virgin Mary holding knitting needles: my favourite is *Our Lady Knitting* by Tommaso da Modena, 1325–75. For hundreds of years, all the best people have been knitting enthusiasts, it seems.

That said, it was not until the nineteenth century that knitting really took hold as a creative pastime. Jane Austen, Charles Dickens and Leo Tolstoy have characters who knit in their novels. The celebrated French romantic artist, William-Adolphe Bouguereau, painted his masterpiece, *The Knitting Girl*, in 1869. Early in the twentieth century, both Virginia Woolf and Agatha Christie created knitting heroines of note. (It is clear that Miss Marple does much of her best thinking while knitting.)

In Europe and America, during both the First and the Second World Wars, people at home were encouraged to 'knit for victory'. 'Our boys need sox,' was the line, 'so knit your bit.' In the 1930s, between the wars, people knitted for economy as much as style, to help keep themselves warm during the privations of the Depression.

What has been fashionable in knitwear has varied down the years. Once upon a time, the principle items that people knitted were stockings and socks, shawls and scarves, pretty clothes for babies and hardy sweaters for sailors. In the 1920s the future King Edward VIII, then Prince of Wales, made Fair Isle fashionable wearing knitted jumpers to play golf. His Royal Highness also wore knitted ties. In the 1950s Hollywood royalty – including Marilyn Monroe, Audrey Hepburn and Grace Kelly (who went on to become European royalty as Princess Grace of Monaco) – wore knitted 'twin sets', a matching cardigan and pullover made of wool or cashmere.

It was in the 1950s that I first started knitting. As a cub scout of six or seven I was taught to knit and awarded a knitting badge as proof of my skill. In the 1960s, at school and university, I wore outsize pullovers and cardigans – a student uniform of sorts. In the early 1970s I founded the National Scrabble Championships and, on the day of the finals, a friend brought me a hand-knitted Scrabble jumper to wear. It was a bright yellow jersey that featured a full-colour life-sized Scrabble board emblazoned on the chest. The garment caused quite a sensation on the day and, in a way, changed my life.

From that day on, colourful jumpers became my professional trademark. Through the 1980s I appeared regularly on British television and when I did I always wore colourful knitwear. Others did, too, of course, but no one else on TV had jumpers quite like mine – or quite so many of them. I had *hundreds*. For the most part, I designed them myself and made sure that I had them for all occasions – featuring hearts for Valentine's Day, bunnies for Easter, daffodils for St David's Day, Shakespeare on his birthday, Winnie the Pooh on mine, the Stars and Stripes on 4 July, ghosts and witches for Halloween... I had at least one different jumper for every day of the year. And I had them for different times of the day, too: ones featuring boiled eggs (and fried eggs) to wear at breakfast and an assortment of *trompe l'oeil* evening jackets for nights out on the town.

In 1990 I gave up television for politics. After a dozen years popping up on game shows like *All Star Secrets*, *The Railway Carriage Game*, *Give Us A Clue*, *Babble* and *Blankety-Blank*, and seven years as a regular in Dictionary Corner on *Countdown* and three mornings a week on the sofa at Britain's first commercial breakfast station, TV-am, I put away my bright knitwear and put on sober grey business suits instead. I became the Member of Parliament for the city of Chester. John Major was the prime minister then. Grey was the order of the day.

Once I had become a politician I assumed I could leave the jolly jumpers behind. Wrong. In my constituency, whenever I did my best to seem statesman-like, the local newspaper would manage to come up with another old photograph of me in a fun knit with which to adorn its front page. At Westminster, I was appointed to the standing committee overseeing the legislation to privatise Britain's railways. Leading for the opposition on the committee was John Prescott, MP. Whenever I got up to speak, he muttered in my direction: 'Woolly jumper! Woolly jumper!' Eventually I had to point out to him that the joy of a woolly jumper is that you can take it off at will, whereas the blight of a woolly mind is that you are lumbered with it for life.

Of course, Mr Prescott got the last laugh because, in time, he became deputy prime minister and is now wrapped in ermine and seated in the House of Lords. But my jumpers had their political advantages, too. Because I was the jumper man I was recognisable. In the constituency people knew who I was – and not every MP is known to his or her constituents. I was visible and accountable. And I could put my jumpers to work in aid of good causes. I gave them away by the drawer-full to raise money for charity. I remember that the novelist Jeffrey Archer auctioned one off for £1,000. And the Duchess of Westminster, married to one of the richest men in the land, generously bought another for £2,000.

Some of my jumpers sold rather well at auction because the best of them were pretty classy. These were the ones specially made for me by George Hostler, who was both a wonderful teacher (the head of design at Leicester Polytechnic, now De Montfort University) and a knitwear designer of note. His other clients included Elton John and Diana, Princess of Wales. I first saw one of George's jumpers on display in a boutique in Kensington. I bought the jumper and got hold of George's number and so our partnership was born. It was not an equal partnership: George had genius, I just had fun ideas. I would conjure up a notion for a novelty knit, doodle it on a piece of paper, with colour suggestions, and pop it in the post to George in Leicester. Within forty-eight hours, he would call me to tell me he was putting the finished garment on the train and I could pick it up from the parcel office at St Pancras Station in the morning. The jumpers in this collection are almost all ones I created either with George or with my alternate partner-in-wool, the brilliant Linda O'Brien.

For a decade I wore novelty knitwear by day and night. (I even had a red-and-white-striped knitted nightgown – with knitted nightcap to match.) My wife wore the knitwear, too, and so did our children. The jumpers we wore at home were a little less loud than the outrageous ones I wore on stage when I appeared in pantomime, but they were still distinctive. I published knitting books and magazines. I judged knitting competitions. I opened knitting shows. For a few years I was director of a chain of hand-knitting wool shops. I was 'the jumping Jack Flash of jolly jumpers' (*The Sun*) and happy to be so.

And then it stopped. From the day I went into politics in 1990 until the day I came to the first photoshoot for the book you are holding in

Gyles and Michele Brandreth letting the train take the strain and Joanna Lumley, looking delightfully dotty in the original Wit Knits collection.

your hands now, I wore not one of my colourful wit-knits. Even after I had lost my parliamentary seat and returned to television, I kept away from the novelty knitwear and stuck to shirts, ties and suits. Even so, my jumper-wearing days were not forgotten – and, perhaps, not surprisingly. The research shows that when people watch TV, they recall 83 per cent of what they see, but only seventeen per cent of what they hear. Everyone has long since forgotten anything I ever said, but quite a few still have a distant memory of what I once wore. Indeed, even today, three decades on from my jumper-wearing heyday, I can't walk down the street without someone asking me, 'Where's your jumper?'

And, happily, thanks to this book, I now have an answer to give them. '*Here* are my jumpers', I can say – or at least here are my favourites. The book has come about because, suddenly, it seems my kind of fun jumper is back in vogue. In 2013, the BBC beat a path to my door. They were making a documentary on The Golden Age of Knitting and needed my input.

'Yey!' I cried, 'I'm a style icon.'

'I wouldn't go that far, dad,' said my daughter, Saethryd. 'Let's just say that some folk think some of your jumpers are fun.'

'And knitting's cool again?'

'Well, dad, Julia Roberts is knitting. Cameron Diaz is knitting. Winona Ryder is knitting.'

So knitting is cool. And good for the soul, too, apparently. Saethryd can tell you more about that in her introduction. All I want you to know is that these jumpers were fun to create, are fun to knit, and fun to wear. Best of all, they will look even better on you than they ever did on me.

Introduction by Saethryd Brandreth

And so here it is. Finally. The moment I stop running away from my childhood, the moment I embrace the past, the moment I fully ride on my father's famous coat/jumper tails, cash in on his celebrity and publish a book, not only with him, but about one of the most cringey skeletons in the sweater-stuffed closet of my childhood. (Actually, if you are looking for a fab skeleton jumper to put in your closet, look no further than page 130.)

Yes, dear readers, dear friends, dear knitters, this is the moment I face the spectre of the novelty jumper.

I'm not ashamed to be here, I'm not embarrassed; on the contrary, I am positively bursting with pullover pride. Why? Because not only is this book raising money for a fantastic cause, Women for Women International, but because Novelty Knits are finally hip. They're wearing them in Williamsburg, New York, Portland, Oregon and Fitzroy, Melbourne; they're wearing them in Shoreditch, Dalston and Whitstable; they're wearing them in Riga, Sodermalm and Amsterdam-Noord.

A few months ago I found myself rummaging through the cardboard box of jumpers that had lain untouched in the attic since the late eighties, pulling the bulldog jumper (page 44) out of its hermetically sealed plastic wrapping and over my head, and thinking, 'This works'.

I never thought this moment would come. What was the tipping point? For me, it has to be the novelty Christmas knit. Yes, there has been a return to the retro over the past few years, a new-found love of craft (there are now over 1,500 Stitch 'n' Bitch groups in over 289 cities worldwide), thrift store chic, and ugly shoes. Designer clothes look crass when so many are struggling, as does looking like you care too much, or that you bought your style lock, stock and barrel marketed to you from the pages of a fashion magazine; and, of course, we must give more than a nod to Sarah Lund in *The Killing*. But it is with the renaissance of the festive jumper that the novelty knit has really come into its own.

When Colin Firth, as Mr Darcy, turned round to Bridget Jones in the 2001 film to reveal he was wearing a reindeer jumper that his Mum had bought him, it was endearing, yes, but a sign that he had his finger on the sartorial pulse? No.

Who could have predicted that a decade later Snoop Dogg, Cheryl Cole, Harry Styles and Kanye West, among others, would have been seen sporting novelty knits with pride and such aplomb?

We are doing this book for fun, for our love of jumpers, of nostalgia and knitting, but we are also doing it for to raise money for Women for

Women International. This fantastic organisation, founded by Zainab Salbi, supports women in war-torn regions with emotional and financial aid, job skills training, rights education and small business assistance. Through a year-long program, women whose lives and communities have been torn apart by war are educated and empowered, giving them the skills and resources they need to rebuild their lives. We are thrilled to be able to help their work in whatever way we can. Each woman that Women for Women International helps has their own individual story to tell and we encourage you to find out more about them, their stories and this incredible organisation. For more information and details of how you can help, womenforwomen.org.uk is a great place to start.

In this book you will find some fabulous sweaters being worn by some equally fabulous people: writers and filmmakers, actors and archeologists, family and friends. Given the work of Women for Women International it was important to us that we get some impressive ladies involved. From Joanna Lumley to Jane Asher to Justine Roberts, these are women who motivate us, inspire us, make us laugh and look 'darn' good in a novelty knit. They range from globally famous faces of stage and screen to faces familiar only to us, but all our models are fascinating, charming, gorgeous people to whom we are truly grateful. They came to our aid, they came for the cause, they posed, they pouted, they hammed it up (somewhat literally in the case of Martha and the pig jumper on page 22) and put on some of the finest knits designed either side of the twenty-first century.

Of course, nothing lasts forever. The novelty knit has now gone beyond the ironic to the iconic. It has hit the mainstream, and so time, tide and fashion dictate that there may only be a brief window in which you can walk down Shoreditch High Street in a jumper that actually has a tail on it. We say embrace that window, put on your fluorescent pink poodle-adorned mohair number, and when that time has passed, get busy knitting one of the many patterns in these pages that are as tasteful, as they are timeless. (I, for one, would wear the cherries sweater on page 68 any day of the week.)

Remember – a novelty jumper is for life, not just for Christmas.

Bear necessity

I've had a life-long love affair with teddy bears. Jim Henson gave me the original Fozzie Bear, Michael Bond gave me the first TV Paddington Bear and I was a friend of the real Christopher Robin, so I can say that I have shaken the hand that held the paw of the original Winnie the Pooh. You can see the Brandreth family's teddy bear collection for free at the Polka Theatre in Wimbledon, South London and you can wear our favourite teddy bear jumper as soon as you have finished knitting it.

MEASUREMENTS

To fit chest/bust: 87(92:97:102:107)cm
Length from shoulder: 61(65:67:69:71)cm
Sleeve length: 49(49:50:51:51)cm
Figures in brackets refer to the larger sizes.
Where only one figure is given this refers to all sizes.

MATERIALS

9(9:10:11:11) x 50g balls of 4-ply yarn in main shade – pink (A)
2 x 50g balls in contrast shade – beige (B)
Small amounts of contrast shades – light brown (C) and black (D)
1 pair each of 2.75mm and 3.25mm knitting needles
The quantities of yarn given are based on average requirements and are therefore approximate.

TENSION

28 sts and 36 rows to 10cm square on 3.25mm needles (or size needed to obtain given tension).

ABBREVIATIONS

alt = alternate; beg = beginning; cont = continue; dec = decrease; foll = following; inc = increase; K = knit; P = purl; patt = pattern; rem = remaining; rep = repeat; RS = right side; st(s) = stitch(es); st st = stocking stitch; tbl = through back of loop; tog = together; WS = wrong side.

BACK

With 2.75mm needles and A, cast on 128(132:140:148:152) sts. Work in K2, P2 rib for 7cm.
Change to 3.25mm needles and starting with a K row, work in st st.
Cont straight until work measures 42(46:48: 49:51)cm from beg, ending with a P row.

Shape armholes

Inc 1 st at both ends of the next and every foll 10th row, 6 times. [142(146:154:162:166) sts.]
Work 5(7:7:9:9) rows straight.

Shape shoulders

Cast off 6(6:6:7:7) sts at beg of next 14 rows and 5(6:9:6:7) sts at beg of next 2 rows.
Leave rem 48(50:52:52:54) sts on a stitch holder.

FRONT

Work as given for back until work measures 8(11:14:14:16)cm from beg, ending with a P row.
Next row: K31(33:37:41:43) sts, K 1st row of the patt from the chart, K to end of row.
Next row: P32(34:38:42:44) sts, P 2nd row of the patt from the chart, P to end of row.
Cont working rows of patt from chart as placed.
At the same time: When work measures same as back to armholes, ending with a P row, shape armholes.

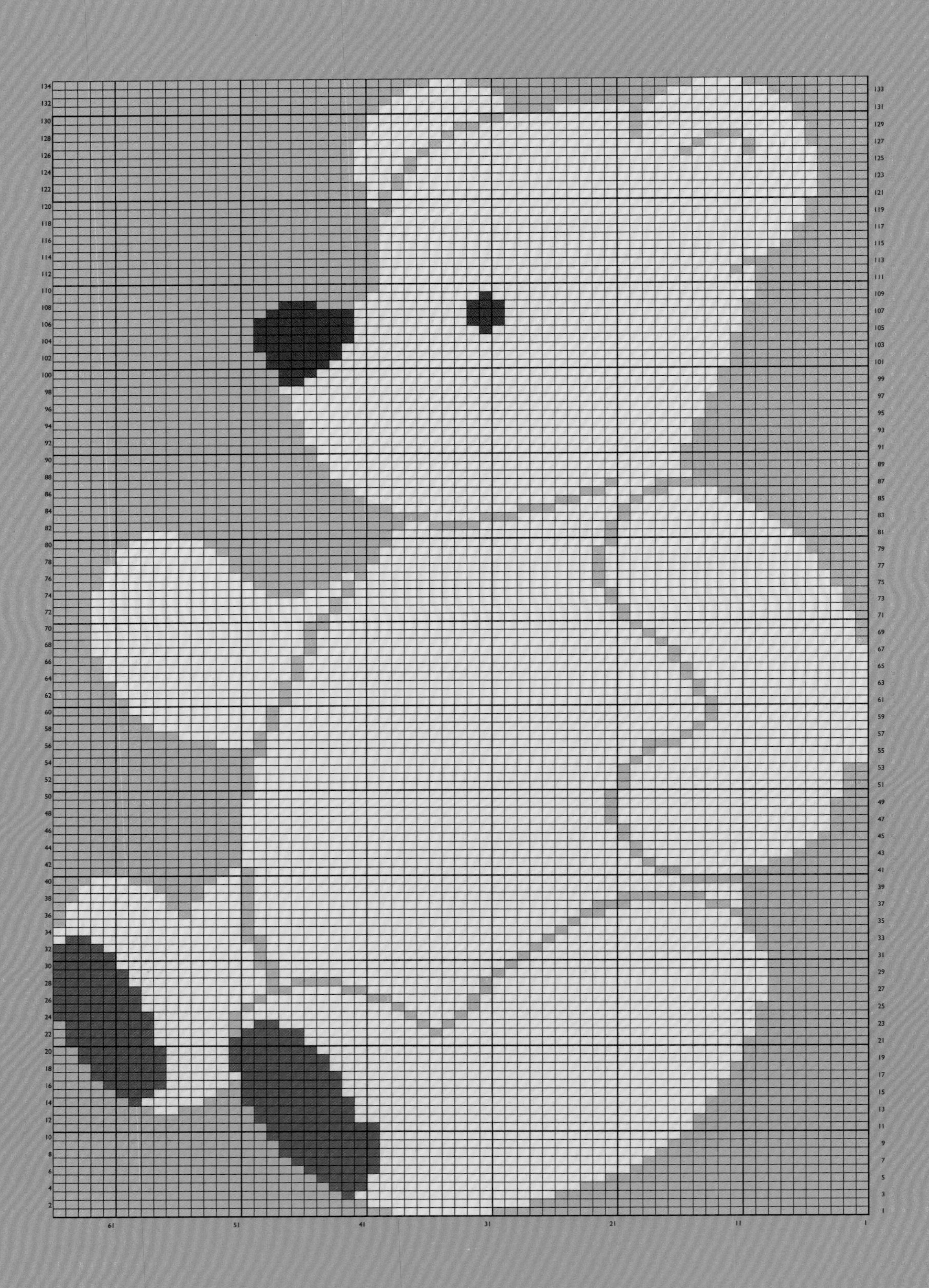

Shape armholes

Inc 1 st at both ends of next and every foll 10th row, 6 times.

At the same time: When work measures 56(60:62:64:66)cm from beg, shape neck.

Shape neck

With RS of work facing, K57(59:62:66:67) sts, turn, leave rem sts on a spare needle.

* Dec 1 st at neck edge on the next 12 rows.

Work straight until length measures same as back to shoulder, ending at armhole edge.

Shape shoulders

Cast off 6(6:6:7:7) sts at beg of next and foll 6 alt rows. Work 1 row. Cast off 5(6:9:6:7) sts.

With RS of work facing, slip next 24(26:28:28:30) sts onto a stitch holder.

Rejoin yarn to next st and K to end of row.

Complete to match first side from * to end.

SLEEVES (both alike)

With 2.75mm needles and A, cast on 64(64:68:68:72) sts. Work in K2, P2 rib for 8cm. On the last row inc 48(48:48:52:52) sts evenly. [112(112:116:120:124) sts.]

Change to 3.25mm needles and starting with a K row, work in st st.

Cont straight until work measures 49(49:50:51:51)cm from beg.

Cast off.

A Pink

B Beige

C Light brown

D Black

NECKBAND

Sew up left shoulder seam.

With 2.75mm needles and RS of work facing, pick up and knit 48(50:52:52:54) sts from back neck, 24 sts from left side neck, 24(26:28:28:30 sts from centre front and 24 sts from right side neck. [120(124:128:128:132) sts.]

Work in K2, P2 rib for 5cm. Cast off loosely in rib.

TO MAKE UP

Press work according to yarn instructions, omitting ribbing.

Sew up right shoulder and neckband.

Fold neckband in half and sew down on WS.

Sew in sleeves. Sew up side and sleeve seams.

Ducks in a row

If it looks like a duck, walks like a duck and talks like a duck, it's probably… a jumper with a row of flying ducks on it, of course! But seriously, you'd be quackers not to fall for this design with its retro flying ducks motif.

MEASUREMENTS

To fit chest/bust: 87(92:97:102:107)cm
Length: 57(58.5:61:63.5:66)cm
Sleeve length: 46.5(48.5:49.5:51:52)cm
Figures in brackets refer to the larger sizes.
Where only one figure is given this refers to all sizes.

MATERIALS

9(10:10:11:11) x 50g balls of DK yarn in main shade – grey (A)
1 x 50g ball of DK yarn in each of contrast shades – brown (B), dark blue (C), mid blue (D), light blue (E)
Small amount of contrast shade – yellow (F)
3 beads for eyes
1 pair each of 3.25mm and 4mm knitting needles
The quantities of yarn given are based on average requirements and are therefore approximate.

TENSION

22 stitches and 30 rows to 10cm square over st st on 4mm needles (or size needed to obtain given tension).

ABBREVIATIONS

alt = alternate; **beg** = beginning; **cont** = continue; **dec** = decrease; **foll** = following; **inc** = increase; **K** = knit; **P** = purl; **patt** = pattern; **rem** = remaining **rep** = repeat; **RS** = right side; **st(s)** = stitch(es); **st st** = stocking stitch; **tog** = together; **WS** = wrong side.

FRONT

With 3.25mm needles and A, cast on 80(84:88:92:96) sts. Work in K1, P1 rib for 4cm.
Change to 4mm needles.
Inc 14(16:18:20:22) sts evenly across row. [94(100:106:112:118) sts.]
Next row: P.
Work in st st for 0(1:2:3:4)cm *.

Place chart *(chart is worked three times)*

Next row: K5(8:11:14:17) sts, working in st st, K 1st row of patt from chart, K to end of row.
Next row: P47(50:53:56:59) sts, P 2nd row of patt from chart, P to end of row.
Cont working rows of patt from chart as placed.
Work a further 6 rows of st st.
Next row: K26(29:32:35:38) sts, K 1st row of patt from chart, K to end.
Next row: P26(29:32:35:38) sts, work 2nd row of chart, P to end.
Cont working rows of patt from chart as placed.
Work a further 6 rows of st st.
Next row: K47(50:53:56:59) sts, K 1st row of patt from chart, K to end.
Next row: P5(8:11:14:17) sts, work 2nd row of chart, P to end.
Cont in st st until work measures 50.5(52:54.5:57:59.5)cm, ending with a WS row.

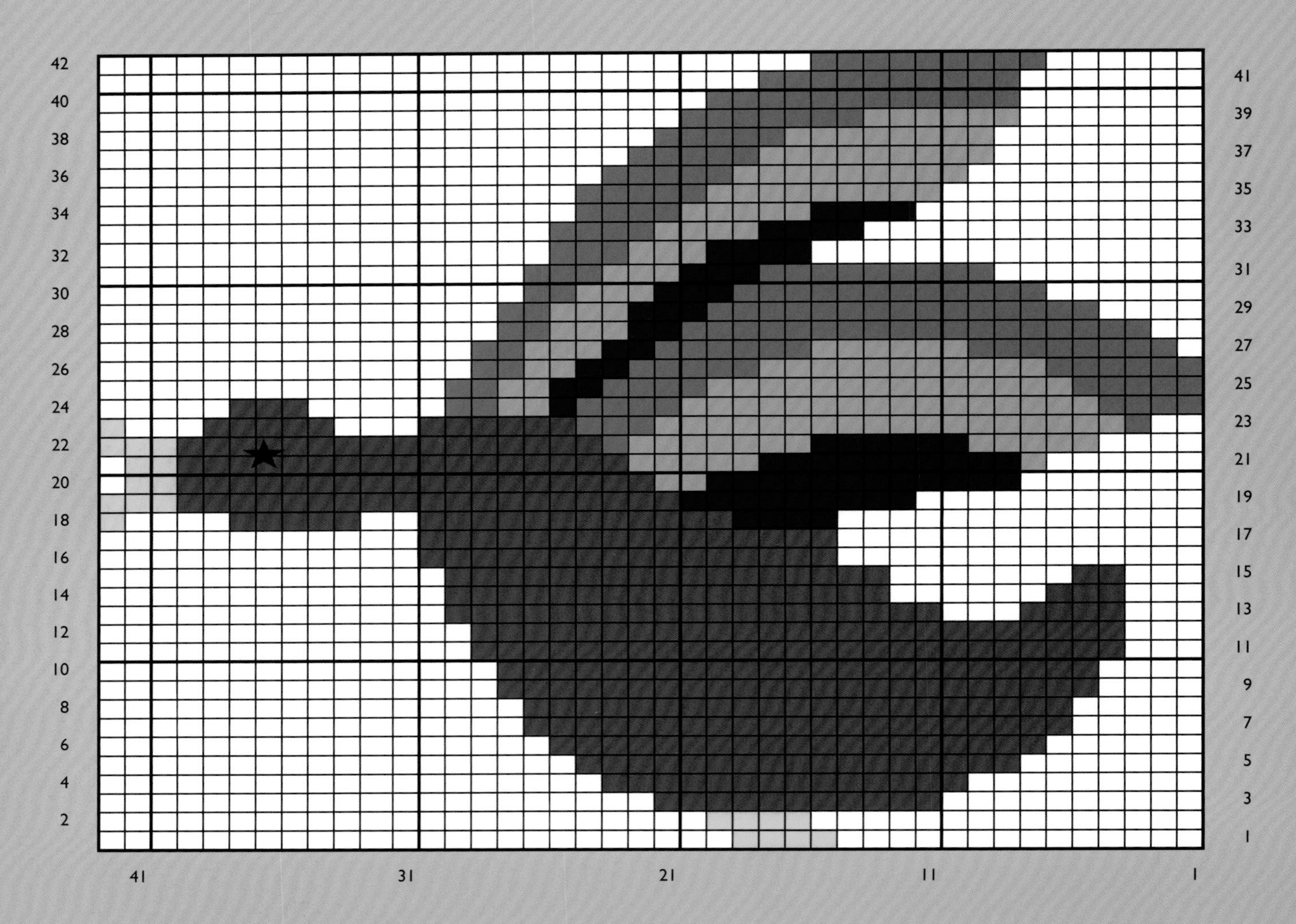

- **A** Grey
- **B** Brown
- **C** Dark blue
- **D** Mid blue
- **E** Light blue
- **F** Yellow
- ★ Place bead

Shape front neck

Next row: K40(43:46:49:52) sts, turn and cont on this first set of sts only, placing rem sts onto a stitch holder.
** Dec 1 st at neck edge on every row until 30(33:36:39:42) sts remain.
Now cont straight until work measures 57(58.5:61:63.5:66)cm.
Cast off all stitches fairly loosely.
Return to rem stitches and slip first 14 sts onto a stitch holder. With RS facing, rejoin yarn to rem sts and K to end of row. Now work as for first side from ** to end.

BACK

Work as for front to *.
Cont straight in st st until work measures 55.5(57:59.5:62:64.5)cm, ending with a WS row.

Shape back neck

Next row: K35(38:41:44:47) sts, turn and cont on this first set of sts only, placing rem sts onto a stitch holder.
*** Dec 1 st at neck edge on next 4 rows.
Cast off rem 30(33:36:39:42) sts fairly loosely.
Return to rem sts and slip first 24 sts onto a stitch holder. With RS facing, rejoin yarn to rem sts and patt to end of row.
Now work as for first side from *** to end.

SLEEVES (both alike)

With 3.25mm needles and A, cast on 46(48:50:52:54) sts and work in K1, P1 rib for 4cm.
Change to 4mm needles.
Inc row: K, inc 20 sts evenly across row. [66(68:70:72:74) sts.]
Next row: P.
Cont in st st and inc 1 st at each end of 5th row and then every foll 6th row until there are 94(100:104:110:114) sts on the needle.
Now work straight in st st until sleeve measures 46.5(48.5:49.5:51:52)cm from cast-on edge, ending with a WS row.
Cast off stitches fairly loosely.

NECKBAND

Join right shoulder seam.
With 3.25mm needles and A and RS facing, pick up and knit 18 sts down left front neck, knit 14 sts from stitch holder, pick up and knit 18 sts up right front neck and 5 sts down right back neck, knit 24 sts from stitch holder and finally pick up and knit 5 sts up left back neck. [84 sts.]
Work in K1, P1 rib for 2.5cm.
Cast off fairly loosely ribwise.

TO MAKE UP

Sew on beads for eyes.
Join left shoulder and neckband.
Measure and mark 22(23:24:25.5:26.5)cm each side of shoulder seam and sew sleeves between these marks.
Join side and sleeve seams, matching pattern at sides.

Squeak piggy squeak

This porcine pullover is a real delight, with a curly tail on the back that's perfect for tweaking. It is being modelled for us by model student Martha Harlan. Martha is Saethryd's god-daughter and a pupil at Bedales, a school founded in the 1890s with roots in the Arts and Crafts movement of the time. (We think William Morris would have loved our jumpers!)

MEASUREMENTS

To fit chest/bust: 87(92:97:102:107:112)cm
Length: 64(67:69:72:72:72)cm
Sleeve length: 48(48:48:51:51:51))cm
Figures in brackets refer to the larger sizes.
Where only one figure is given this refers to all sizes.

MATERIALS

3(3:3:3:4:4) x 50g balls of DK yarn in 1st colour – dark grey (A).
5(5:6:6:6:6) x 50g balls of DK yarn in 2nd colour – light grey (B)
1 x 50g ball of DK yarn in 3rd colour – pink (C)
Small amount of contrast shade – black (D)
1 pair each of 3.25mm and 4mm knitting needles
1 medium size crochet hook
The quantities of yarn given are based on average requirements and are therefore approximate.

TENSION

22 stitches and 28 rows to 10cm square over st st on 4mm needles (or size needed to obtain given tension).

ABBREVIATIONS

alt = alternate; beg = beginning; cont = continue; dec = decrease; foll = following; inc = increase; K = knit; P = purl; patt = pattern; rem = remaining; rep = repeat; RS = right side; st(s) = stitch(es); st st = stocking stitch; tbl = through back of loop; tog = together; WS = wrong side.

BACK

With 3.25mm needles and A, cast on 82(88:94:98:104:110) sts. Work in K1, P1, rib for 18 rows.
Change to 4mm needles.
Inc row: K6(9:12:14:17:20), inc in next st.
* K3, inc in next st, rep from * to last 7(10:13:15:18:21)sts, K to end of row.
[100(106:112:116:122:128) sts.]
Next row: P.
Now starting with a K row, work 36(36:36:46:46:46) rows straight in st st in A.
Break off A and cont in B as follows:

Place chart

Next row (RS facing): With B, K30(33:36:36:39:42) sts, work across the 40(40:40:44:44:44) sts from 1st row of Chart 1(1:1:2:2:2), then with B, K rem 30(33:36:36:39:42) sts.
Chart is now set. Cont to work the 56(56:56:62:62:62) rows of chart, but DO NOT work the face features. **
When the chart is complete cont straight in st st in B until back measures 62(65:67:70:70:70)cm from cast-on edge, ending with a WS row.

Shape back neck

Next row: K35(38:41:43:46:49) sts, turn and cont on this first set of sts only, placing rem sts onto a stitch holder.
*** Dec 1 st at neck edge on next 3 rows.

Cast off rem 32(35:38:40:43:46) sts fairly loosely.
Return to rem sts and slip first 30 sts onto a stitch holder.
With RS facing, rejoin yarn to rem sts and K to end of row.
Now work as for first side from *** to end.

FRONT

Work as for back to **, but WORK ALL face features as shown on chart. When chart is complete cont straight in st st in B until front measures 56(59:61:64:64:64)cm from cast-on edge, ending with a WS row.

Shape front neck

Next row: K42(45:48:50:53:56) sts, turn and cont on this first set of sts only, placing rem sts onto a stitch holder.
**** Dec 1 st at neck edge on every row until 32(35:38:40:43:46) sts remain.
Now cont straight until front measures the same as back to shoulder cast-off edge, ending with a WS row.
Cast off all sts fairly loosely.
Return to rem sts and slip first 16 sts onto a stitch holder. With RS facing, rejoin yarn to rem sts and K to end of row.
Now work as for first side from **** to end.

SLEEVES (both alike)

With 3.25mm needles and A, cast on 44 sts, and work in K1, P1 rib for 18 rows.

Change to 4mm needles.

Inc row: K2, inc in next st. * K1, inc in next st, rep from * to last 3 sts, K to end. [64 sts.]

Now starting with a P row, work in st st in A.

At the same time: Inc 1 st at each end of every foll 6th row until there are 74 sts on the needle, ending with a WS row.

Change to B and cont to inc as before on every foll 6th row until there are 94(94:94:100:100:100) sts on the needle.

Now work straight in st st in B until sleeve measures 48(48:48:51:51:51)cm from cast-on edge, ending with a WS row.

Cast off all sts fairly loosely.

NECKBAND

Join right shoulder seam.

With 3.25mm needles and A and RS facing, pick up and knit 21 sts down left front neck, knit 16 sts from stitch holder, pick up and knit 21 sts up right front neck, knit 4 sts down right back neck, knit 30 sts from stitch holder and finally pick up and knit 4 sts up left back neck. [96 sts.]

Work in K1, P1 rib for 12 rows.

Cast off fairly loosely ribwise.

TO MAKE UP

Press according to ball band instructions.

Join left shoulder and neckband seam. Fold neckband in half to inside and slip stitch loosely in position. Measure and mark 23(23:23:24:24:24)cm each side of shoulder seam and sew sleeves between these marks. Join side and sleeve seams.

Piggy tail

With the medium size crochet hook and C, make 20 chains, then work double crochet st into every loop, starting at the loop nearest the needle. The tail will curl up as you work. Tie ends together and sew in place on back.

Snakes alive

They say that time, tide and the receding hairline wait for no man, but the same can't be said of this fabulous snake jumper – a unique Brandreth/Hostler creation, which looks just as dapper (and dangerous) today as it did when it was first photographed back in 1982. (Pity the same can't be said for the chap modelling it. This is what happens when you get talking to the wrong types in the Garden of Eden.)

MEASUREMENTS

To fit chest/bust: 86(91:96:101:107:112)cm
Length from shoulder: 63(66:69:71:71:71)cm
Sleeve length: 48(48:48:51:51:51)cm
Figures in brackets refer to the larger sizes.
Where only one figure is given this refers to all sizes.

MATERIALS

11(11:12:12:12:13) x 50g balls of Aran yarn in main shade – navy (A)
2 x 50g balls in each of contrast shades – green (B) and yellow (C)
Small amount in each of white (D) and red (E)
1 pair each of 4mm and 5mm knitting needles
2 buttons or beads for eyes
2 stitch holders
The quantities of yarn given are based on average requirements and are therefore approximate.

TENSION

18 sts and 22 rows to 10cm square over st st on 5mm needles (or size needed to obtain given tension).

ABBREVIATIONS

beg = beginning; **cont** = continue; **dec** = decrease; **foll** = following; **inc** = increase; **K** = knit; **P** = purl; **patt** = pattern; **rem** = remaining; **rep** = repeat; **RS** = right side; **st(s)** = stitch(es); **st st** = stocking stitch; **tog** = together; **WS** = wrong side.

BACK

With 4mm needles and A, cast on 66(70:74:80:84:88) sts and work in K1, P1 rib for 16 rows.
Change to 5mm needles.
Inc row: K2(4:6:9:11:13), inc in next st, *K3, inc in next st, rep from * to last 3(5:7:10:12:14) sts, K to end of row. [82(86:90:96:100:104) sts.]
Next row: P.
Now starting with a K row, work straight in st st for 2(8:14:20:20:20) rows. **

Place chart

Now starting with the 1st row, work in st st from Chart 1, working between appropriate lines for size required. Cont as set until the 38 rows of chart are complete.
Now work straight in st st in A for a further 48 rows, ending with a WS row.

Place chart

Now starting with the 1st row, work in st st from Chart 2, working between appropriate lines for size required until 28th row of chart has been completed, ending with a WS row.

Shape back neck

Next row (29th row of chart): Patt 31(33:35:38:40:42) sts, turn and cont on this first set of sts only, placing rem sts on a stitch holder.

*** Keeping chart correct, dec 1 st at neck edge on next 3 rows. (32nd row of chart complete.)

Cast off rem 28(30:32:35:37:39) sts fairly loosely.

Return to rem sts and slip first 20 sts onto a stitch holder. With RS facing, rejoin yarn to rem sts and patt to end of row.

Now work as for first side from *** to end.

FRONT

Work as for back to **.

Place chart

Now starting with the 1st row, work in st st from Chart 3, working between appropriate lines for size required.

Cont straight working from chart until 102nd row of chart has been worked, ending with a WS row.

CHART 1

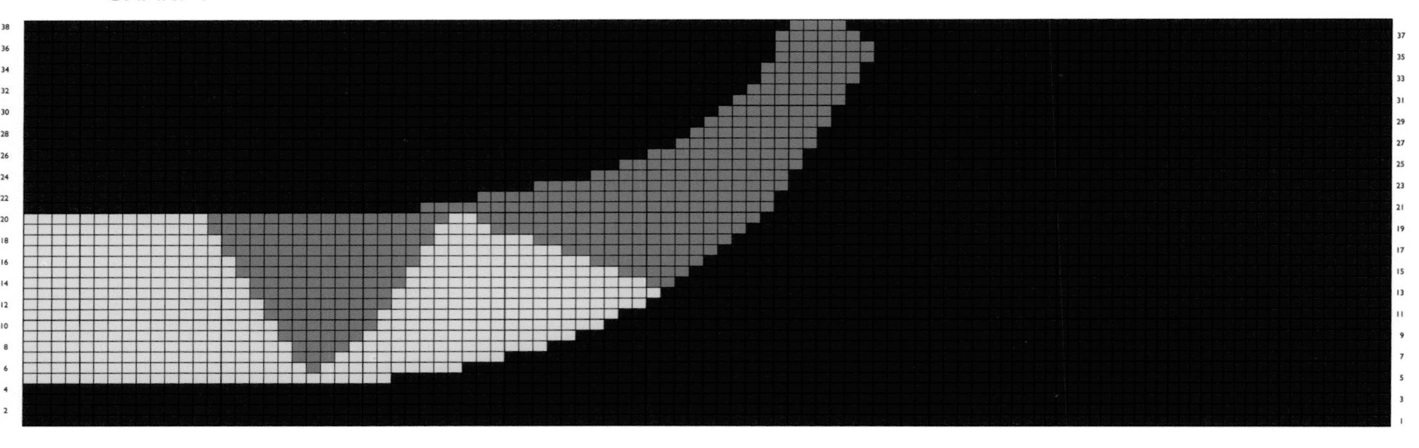

CHART 2

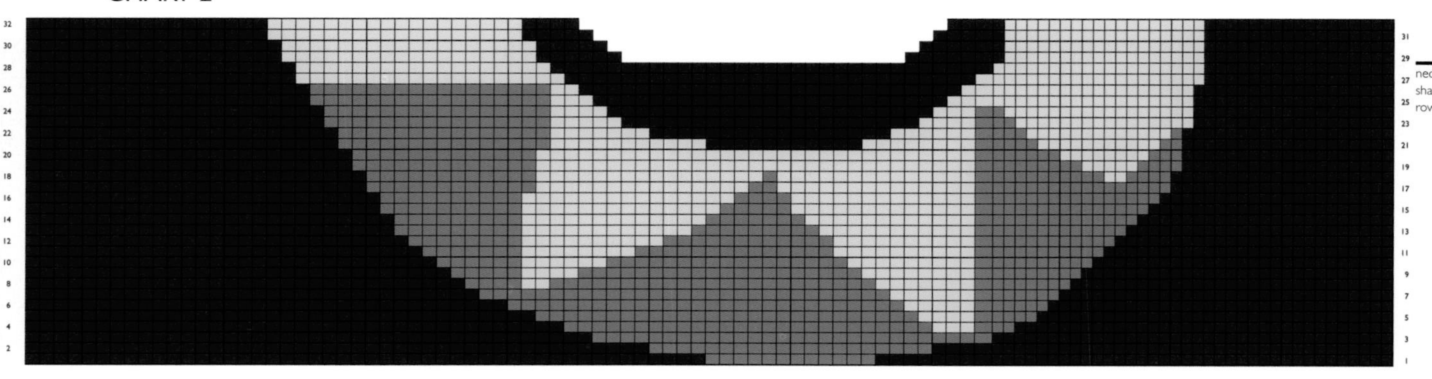

CHART 3

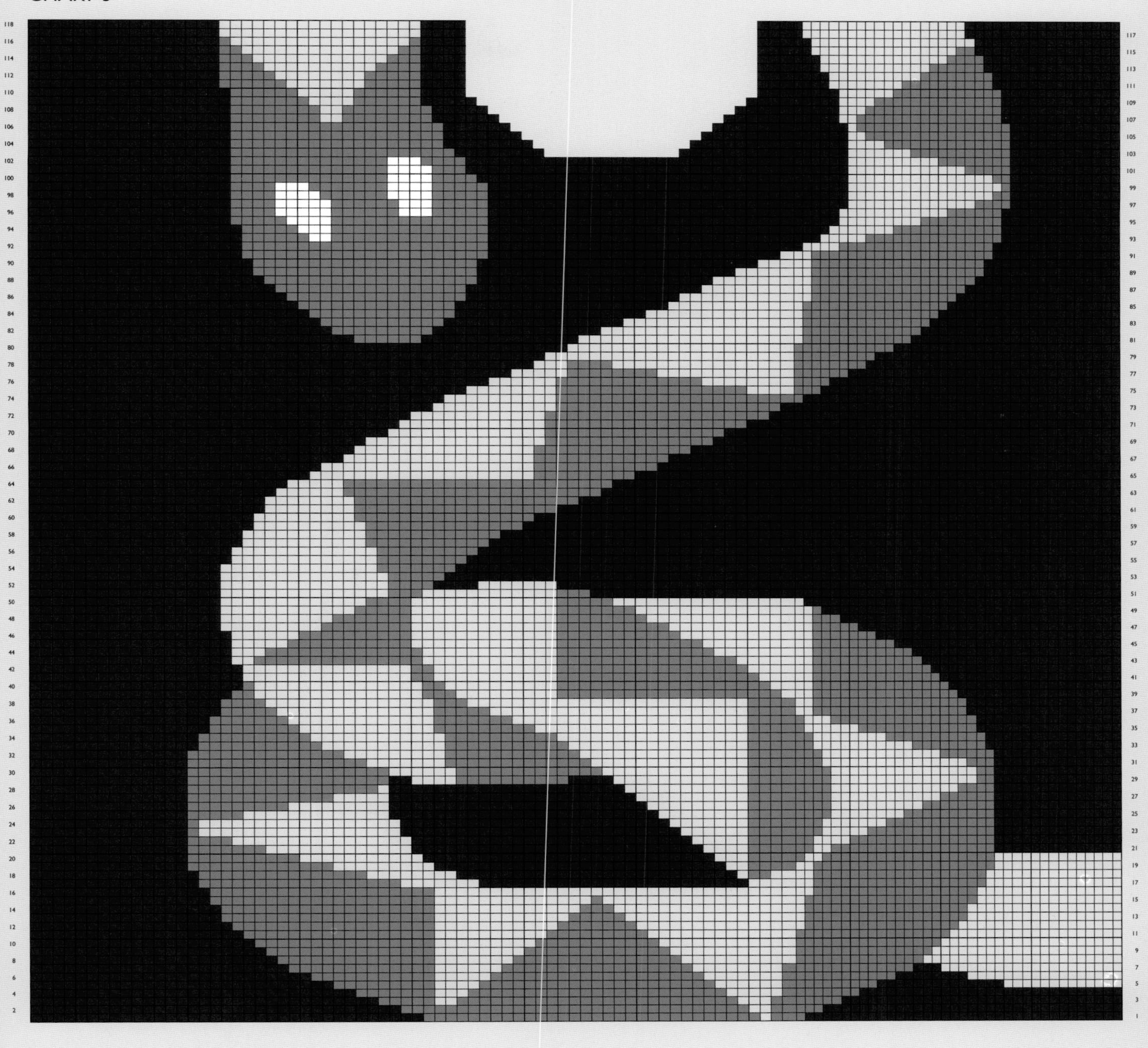

A Navy
B Green
C Yellow
D White

Snakes alive, is that really Gyles in 1985?

Shape front neck

Next row (103rd) row of chart: Patt 35(37:39:42:44:46) sts, turn and cont on this first set of sts only, placing rem sts on a stitch holder.
**** Keeping chart correct, dec 1 st at neck edge on every row until 28(30:32:35:37:39) sts remain.
Now cont straight until chart is complete (118th row worked).
Cast off all sts fairly loosely. (Front measures same as back.)
Return to rem sts and slip first 12 sts onto a stitch holder. With RS facing, rejoin yarn to rem sts and patt to end of row.
Now work as for first side from **** to end.

SLEEVES (both alike)

With 4mm needles and A, cast on 36 sts and work in K1, P1 rib for 14 rows.
Change to 5mm needles.
Inc row: *K1, inc in next 2 sts, rep from * to end. [60 sts.]
Now starting with a P row, cont in st st and A, inc 1 st at each end of every foll 6th row until there are 80(80:80:88:88:88) sts on the needle.
Now cont straight in st st until sleeve measures 48(48:48:51:51:51)cm from cast-on edge, ending with a WS row.
Cast off all sts fairly loosely.

NECKBAND

Join right shoulder seam matching patt.
With 4mm needles and A and RS facing, pick up and knit 17 sts down left front neck, knit 12 sts from stitch holder, pick and knit 17 sts up right front neck, knit 4 sts down right back neck, knit 20 sts from stitch holder and finally pick up and knit 4 sts up left back neck. [74 sts.]
Work in K1, P1 rib for 10 rows.
Cast off fairly loosely ribwise.

TO MAKE UP

Press according to ball band instructions.
Join left shoulder and neckband seam matching patt. Fold neckband in half to inside and slip stitch loosely in position. Measure and mark 24(24:24:27:27:27)cm each side of shoulder seam and sew sleeves between these marks. Sew beads or buttons in place for eyes.

To make tongue

With E and 12 strands of yarn, tightly plait for 3cm, then cont plait in 2 bunches of 6 strands. When these are also 3cm secure both ends with a knot.
Sew tongue in place.
Join side and sleeve seams, matching patt.

Divine dachshund

The temperament of the sausage dog is described as lively, playful, devoted, clever, stubborn and courageous. Not unlike our lovely model, comedienne Shappi Khorsandi. This modern-day design by Sarah Kim is an instant classic.

MEASUREMENTS

To fit chest/bust: 81(86:91:97:102:107:112)cm
Length: 62(63:65:68:71:75:77)cm
Sleeve length: 42(44:46:48:50:52:52)cm
Figures in brackets refer to the larger sizes.
Where only one figure is given this refers to all sizes.

MATERIALS

- 4(4:5:5:6:6:7) x 50g balls of 4-ply yarn in main shade – light grey (MC)
- 1 x 50g ball of 4-ply yarn in each of contrast shades – black (A) and gold (B)
- 1 pair each of 2.75mm and 3.25mm knitting needles
- 2 stitch holders
- 1 stitch marker

The quantities of yarn given are based on average requirements and are therefore approximate.

TENSION

28 stitches and 36 rows to 10cm square over st st on 3.25mm needles (or size needed to obtain given tension).

ABBREVIATIONS

alt = alternate; **beg** = beginning; **cont** = continue; **dec** = decrease; **foll** = following; **inc** = increase; **K** = knit; **K2tog** = knit 2 together; **P** = purl; **P2tog** = purl 2 together; **patt** = pattern; **pm** = place marker; **psso** = pass slipped stitch over; **rem** = remaining; **rep** = repeat; **RS** = right side; **s** = slip; **st(s)** = stitch(es); **st st** = stocking stitch; **tbl** = through back of loop; **tog** = together; **WS** = wrong side.

PLACEMENT OF BACK CHART

Follow pattern for back on page 32 until work measures 15(16:17:19:22:25:26)cm, ending with a WS row.

Next row: Starting at the point indicated for the size you are knitting, K across 97(103:109:115:121:129:135) sts of chart, pm, K across rem 30(32:34:36:38:40:42) sts of row in MC. This row shows placement of chart. Complete 110 rows of chart.
At the same time: Cont working back patt shapings.

BACK

With 2.75mm needles and MC, cast on 127(135:143:151:159:169:177) sts.
Row 1 (RS): *K1, P1, rep from * to last st, K1.
Row 2: P1, *K1, P1, rep from * to end of row.
Work 20 more rows in K1, P1 rib.
Change to 3.25mm needles and proceed as follows:
Row 1: K.
Row 2: P.
Working in st st, cont until back measures 42(43:44:45:46:47:48)cm, ending with a WS row.

Shape armholes

Cast off 8 sts at beg next 2 rows.
[111(119:127:135:143:153:161) sts.]
Row 1: K1, s1, K1, psso, K to last 3 sts, K2tog, K1.
[109(117:125:133:141:151:159) sts.]
Row 2: P1, P2tog, P to last 3 sts, P2tog tbl, P1.
[107(115:123:131:139:149:157) sts.]
Rows 1 and 2 set dec for armholes.
Work 21 rows, dec 1 st as before at each end of next 7 rows, and then on every foll alt row.
[79(87:95:103:111:121:129) sts.]
** Cont in st st without shaping until armhole measures 14(15:16:18:20:22:24)cm, ending with WS row.

Shape back neck

Row 1: K17(21:24:28:30:35:38) sts, turn, leave rem 62(66:71:75:81:86:91) sts on a stitch holder.
Working on these 17(21:24:28:30:35:38) sts only, proceed as follows:
Next row: Dec 1 st at neck edge and P to end with RS facing for next row. [16(20:23:27:29:34:37) sts.]

Shape shoulder

Cast off 4(5:7:8:9:10:11) sts at beg of next and foll alt row.
At the same time: Dec 1 st at neck edge of next 3 rows. [5(7:6:8:8:11:12) sts.]
Work 1 row.
Cast off rem 5(7:6:8:8:11:12) sts.
With RS facing, slip centre 45(45:47:47:51:51:53) sts onto a stitch holder. Rejoin yarn to rem 17(21:24:28:30:35:38) sts and proceed as follows:
Next row: Dec 1 st at neck edge, K to end of row with WS facing for next row.
[16(20:23:27:29:34:37) sts.]
Cast off 4(5:7:8:9:10:11) sts at beg of next and foll alt row.
At the same time: Dec 1 st at neck edge of next 3 rows. [5(7:6:8:8:12:13) sts.]
Work 1 row.
Cast off rem 5(7:6:8:8:12:13) sts.

PLACEMENT OF FRONT CHART

Follow patt for front on page 35 until work measures 15(16:17:19:22:25:26)cm, ending with a WS row.
Next row: K30(32:34:36:38:40:42) sts in MC, pm, K across 97(103:109:115:121:129:135) sts of chart stopping at the point indicated for the size you are working. This row shows placement of chart.

MC Light grey
A Black
B Gold

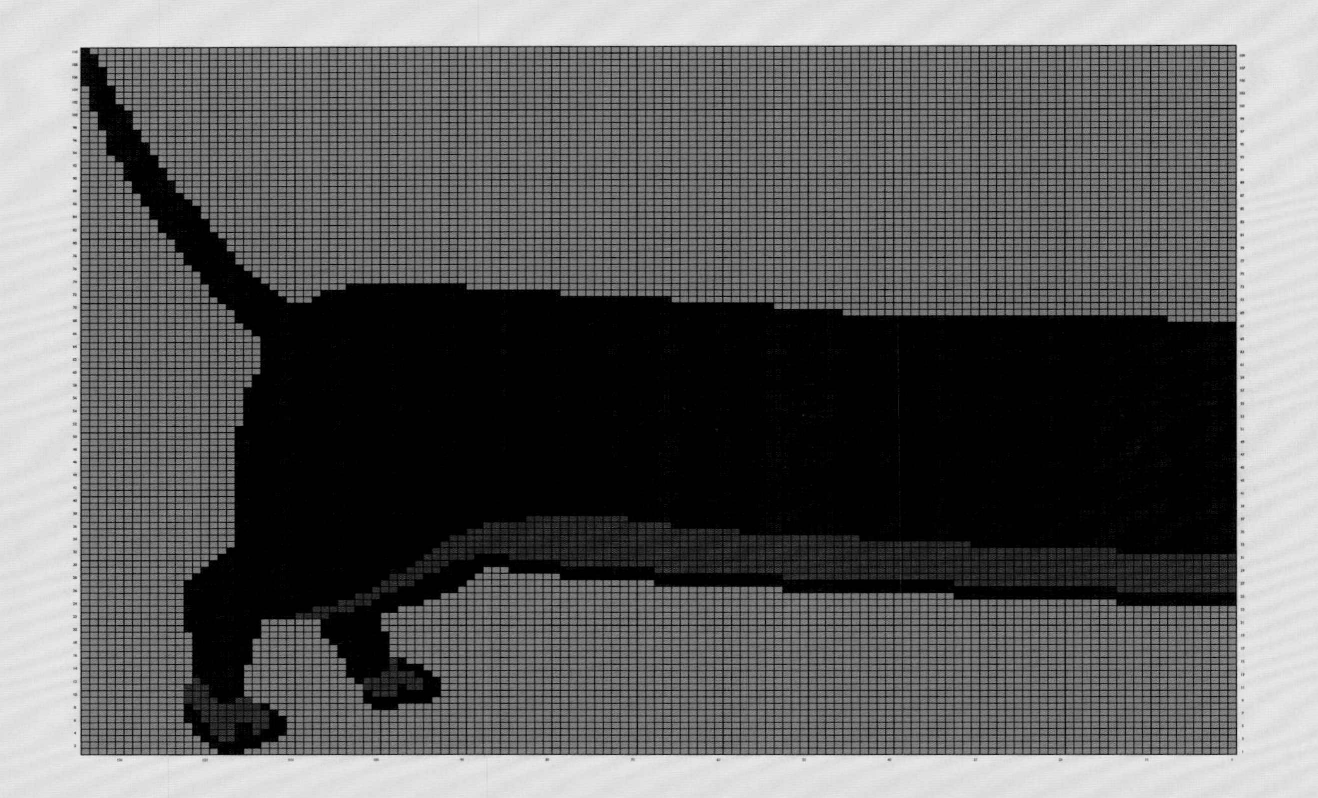

Complete 110 rows of chart.
At the same time: Cont working front pattern shapings.

FRONT

Work as given for Back to **.
Cont in st st without shaping until armhole measures 9(10:11:13:15:17:18.5)cm, ending with WS row.

Shape front neck

Next row: K27(31:34:38:42:45:49), turn, leave rem 52(56:61:65:69:76:80) sts on a stitch holder.
Working on these 27(31:34:38:42:45:49) sts only, proceed as follows:
Work 18 rows, dec 1 st at neck edge of next 10 rows, then on 4 foll alt rows. [13(17:20:24:28:31:35) sts.]
Work 1 row with RS facing for next row.
Cast off 4(5:6:8:9:10:11) sts at beg of next and foll alt row. [5(7:8:8:10:11:13) sts.]
Work 1 row.
Cast off rem 5(7:8:8:10:11:13) sts.
With RS facing, slip centre 25(25:27:27:27:31:31) sts onto a stitch holder. Rejoin yarn to rem 27(31:34:38:42:45:49) sts, and proceed as follows:
Work 18 rows, dec 1 st at neck edge of next 10 rows, then on 4 foll alt rows. [13(17:20:24:28:31:35) sts.]
Work 1 row with WS facing for next row.
Cast off 4(5:6:8:9:10:11) sts at beg of next and foll alt row. [5(7:8:8:10:11:13) sts.]
Work 1 row.
Cast off rem 5(7:8:8:10:11:13) sts.

SLEEVES (both alike)

With 2.75mm needles and MC, cast on 63(65:67:69:73:75:79) sts, work 22 rows in K1, P1 rib.
Change to 3.25mm needles and, working in st st, inc 1 st at each end of 3rd and every foll 4th row to 101(105:109:105:97:95:99) sts, then for every foll 0(0:0:6th:6th:6th:6th) row until 0(0:0:113:117:121:125) sts.
Cont without shaping until sleeve measures 37(39:41:45:49:52:52)cm, or length required, ending with a WS row.

Shape top

Cast off 8 sts at beg of next 2 rows. [85(89:93:97:101:105:109) sts.]
Dec 1 st as before on each end of next 3 rows, then on every foll alt row to 73 sts, then on foll 13 rows, ending with RS facing for next row. [47 sts.]
Cast off 5 sts at beg of next 4 rows.
Cast off rem 27 sts.

NECKBAND

Join right shoulder seam.
With RS facing, using MC and 2.75mm needles, pick up and knit 16(18:18:20:20:20:21) sts evenly along left side of front neck, knit across 25(25:27:27:27:31:31) sts left on stitch holder at front of neck, pick up and knit 16(18:18:20:20:20:21) sts evenly along right side of front neck, pick up and knit 6 sts evenly along right side of back neck, knit across 45(45:47:47:51:51:53) sts left on stitch holder at back of neck, pick up and knit 6 sts evenly along left side of front neck. [114(118:122:126:130:134:138) sts.]
Work 11 rows in K1, P1 rib.
Cast off in rib.

TO MAKE UP

Join left shoulder and neckband seams. Sew in sleeves. Join side and sleeve seams. Weave in all ends. Pin out garment to the measurements given. Cover with damp cloths and leave until dry. See ball band for washing and further care instructions.

Poodle

Pretty in poodle-adorned pink is our lovely chum, yoga teacher and actress Kandy Rohmann. Kandy was personally inspired by Women for Women founder Zainab Salbi to follow her creative passions, as well as raise bucketloads of money for the cause. She has run a 10K, organised film screenings and was even named a Women for Women sponsor of the month. Zainab may have been named one of the most inspirational women in the world by The Economist, but we think Kandy's not doing too badly herself.

MEASUREMENTS

To fit chest/bust: 87(92:97:102)cm
Length: 63(63:64:64)cm
Sleeve length: 41cm
Figures in brackets refer to the larger sizes.
Where only one figure is given this refers to all sizes.

MATERIALS

16(16:18:18) x 25g balls of Sirdar Snowflake Chunky in main shade – pink (A)
2 x 25g balls of Sirdar Snowflake Chunky in contrast shade – white (B)
Small amount of contrast shade – black (C)
1 pair each of 3.75mm and 5mm knitting needles
The quantities of yarn given are based on average requirements and are therefore approximate.

TENSION

14 stitches and 19 rows to 10cm square over st st on 6mm needles (or size needed to obtain given tension).

ABBREVIATIONS

alt = alternate; **beg** = beginning; **cont** = continue; **dec** = decrease; **foll** = following; **inc** = increase; **K** = knit; **P** = purl; **patt** = pattern; **rem** = remaining; **rep** = repeat; **RS** = right side; **st(s)** = stitch(es); **st st** = stocking stitch; **tbl** = through back of loop; **tog** = together; **WS** = wrong side.

BACK

With 3.75mm needles and A, cast on 122 (124: 128:130) sts.
Work in K1, P1 rib for 7cm.
Dec row: Rib 1(5:7:11) sts, * work 2 tog, rib 1, rep from * to last 1(5:7:11) sts, rib to end. [82(86:90:94) sts.]
Change to 6mm needles and starting with a K row, work in st st.
Cont straight until work measures 37cm from beg, ending with a P row.

Shape sleeves

Cast on 4 sts at beg of every row to 162(166:170: 174) sts.
Work straight until work measures 63(63:64:64)cm from beg, ending with a P row.
Cast off 67(69:70:72) sts at beg of next 2 rows, leave rem 28(28:30:30) sts on a holder.

FRONT

Work as given for back until work measures 17cm from beg, ending with a P row.
Next row: K18(20:22:24) sts, K 1st row of patt from chart, K to end of row.
Next row: P17(19:21:23) sts, P 2nd row of patt from chart, P to end of row.
Cont working rows of patt from chart as placed.

Dog lover and author of The Sloane Rovers Handbook, *a must read for every pampered pooch, here is Francesca Findlater (right), sitting pretty in 1986.*

At the same time: When work measures same as back to armholes, ending with a P row, shape sleeves.

Shape sleeves

Work as for back, until work measures 57(57:58:58) cm from beg.

Shape neck

With RS of work facing, K77(79:80:82) sts, turn, leave rem sts on a spare needle.
Cast off 4 sts at beg of next row and 3(3:3:3) sts at beg of foll alt rows.
Work 12 rows straight. Cast off.
With RS of work facing, slip next 8(8:10:10) sts onto a stitch holder. Rejoin yarn to next st and K to end of row. Complete to match first side.

NECKBAND

Sew up left shoulder.
With 3.75mm needles and RS of work facing, pick up and knit 28(28:30:30) sts from back neck, 14 sts from left side neck, 8(8:10:10) sts from centre front, and 14 sts from right side neck. [64(64:66:66) sts.]
Work 4 rows in K1, P1 rib. Cast off loosely in rib.

CUFFS

Sew up right shoulder and neckband with RS of work facing. With 3.75mm needles, pick up and knit 48(48:52:52) sts along lower edge of sleeve. Work in K1, P1 rib for 12cm. Cast off in rib.

TO MAKE UP

Do not press but brush lightly with a damp brush to raise the pile. Sew up side and underarm seams.

A Pink
B White
C Black

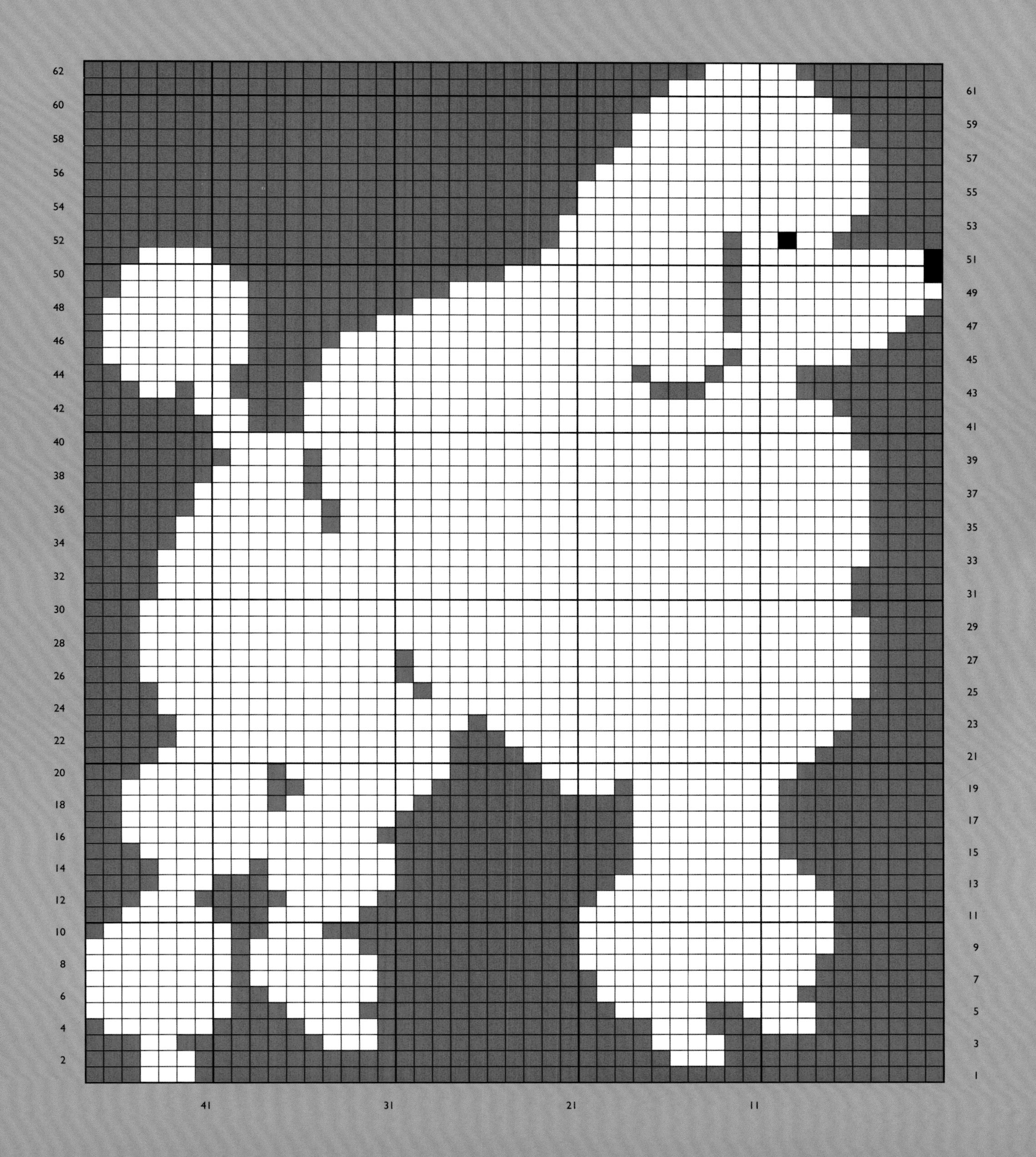

Scaredy cat

Here is Joanna Lumley modelling our absolutely fabulous pussycat jumper. It's the purr-fect knit for Joanna who is a long time vegetarian and passionate about animal rights. We hope you'll be just as keen on our fantastic kitty knit. (The cat is probably in shock as he's just realised he is being modelled by the lovely Miss Lumley.)

MEASUREMENTS

To fit chest/bust: 82(87:92:97:102)cm
Length: 55(57:60:65:68)cm
Sleeve length: 43(46:48:48:49)cm
Figures in brackets refer to the larger sizes.
Where only one figure is given this refers to all sizes.

MATERIALS

5(5:6:7:7) x 50g balls of 4-ply yarn in main shade – blue (MC)
2 x 50g balls of 4-ply yarn in contrast shade – black (A)
Small amounts of contrast shades – fuchsia (B), yellow (C) and red (D)
1 pair each of 2.75mm and 3.25mm knitting needles
The quantities of yarn given are based on average requirements and are therefore approximate.

TENSION

28 sts and 36 rows to 10cm square over st st on 3.25mm needles (or size needed to obtain given tension).

ABBREVIATIONS

alt = alternate; **beg** = beginning; **cont** = continue; **dec** = decrease; **foll** = following; **inc** = increase; **K** = knit; **P** = purl; **patt** = pattern; **rem** = remaining **rep** = repeat; **RS** = right side; **st(s)** = stitch(es); **st st** = stocking stitch; **tog** = together; **WS** = wrong side.

BACK

With 2.75mm needles and MC, cast on 120(126:132:140:148) sts. Work in K2, P2 rib for 6cm. Change to 3.25mm needles and starting with a K row, work in st st. Cont straight until work measures 37(39:42:46:49)cm from beg, ending with a P row.

Shape armholes

Inc 1 st at both ends of next and every foll 10th row, 6 times. [134(140:146:154:160) sts].
Work 5(5:5:7:7) rows straight.

Shape shoulders

Cast off 6(7:7:6:7) sts at beg of next 12(12:12:14:14) rows, and 8(4:6:9:5) sts at beg of next 2 rows.
Leave rem 46(48:50:52:52) sts on a holder.

FRONT

Work as given for back until work measures 15(18:20:24:27)cm from beg, ending with a P row.
Next row: K24(27:30:34:38) sts, K 1st row of patt from chart, K to end of row.
Next row: P25(28:31:35:39) sts, P 2nd row of patt from chart, P to end of row.
Cont working rows of patt from chart as placed.
At the same time: When work measures same as back to armholes, shape armholes.

Shape armholes
Inc 1 st at both ends of next and every foll 10th row, 6 times.
At the same time: When work measures 49(52:55:59:62)cm from beg, shape neck.

Shape neck
With RS of work facing, knit 53(55:57:62:65) sts, turn, leave rem sts on a spare needle.
* Dec 1 st at neck edge on next 11(11:11:12:12) rows. Work straight until length measures same as back to shoulder, ending at armhole edge.

Shape shoulders
Cast off 6(7:7:6:7) sts at beg of next and foll 5(5:5:6:7) alt rows. Work 1 row. Cast off 8(4:6:9:5) sts. With RS of work facing, slip next 24(26:28:28:28) sts onto a stitch holder. Rejoin yarn to next st and K to end of row.
Complete to match first side from * to end.

SLEEVES (both alike)
With 2.75mm needles and MC, cast on 60(64:64:68:68) sts.
Work in K2, P2 rib for 7cm.
On the last row inc 44(48:48:48:48) sts evenly. [104(112:112:116:116) sts].
Change to 3.25mm needles and starting with a K row, work in st st.
Cont straight until work measures 43(46:48:48:49)cm from beg.
Cast off.

MC Blue

A Black

C Yellow

D Red

B Fuchsia

NECKBAND
Sew up left shoulder seam.
With 2.75mm needles and MC, pick up and knit 46(48:50:52:52) sts from back neck, 22(22:22:24:25) sts from left side neck, 24(26:28:28:28) sts from centre front and 22(22:22:24:25) sts from right side neck. [114(118:122:128:130) sts].
Work in K2, P2 rib for 5cm. Cast off loosely in rib.

TO MAKE UP
Press work according to yarn instructions, omitting ribbing.
Sew up right shoulder seam and neckband.
Fold neckband in half and sew down on WS.
Sew in sleeves. Sew up side and sleeve seams.

Bulldog spirit

We Brits are a nation of dog lovers, which is why we've included a whole pack of doggy designs in this book. The Labrador Retriever may have been the most popular pooch in the UK for the last ten years running – in France it's the poodle, in Japan it's the Chihuahua and in Australia it's the Staffordshire Bull Terrier – but, if you ask me, you can't beat the Great British Bulldog.

MEASUREMENTS

To fit chest/bust: 87(92:99:102:107)cm
Length from shoulder: 62(66:69:70:71)cm
Sleeve length: 48cm
Figures in brackets refer to the larger sizes.
Where only one figure is given this refers to all sizes.

MATERIALS

9(9:10:11:11) x 50g balls of 4-ply yarn in main shade – grey (A)
1 x 50g ball in contrast shade – white (B)
Small amount of contrast shade – black (C)
1 pair each of 2.75mm and 3.25mm knitting needles
The quantities of yarn given are based on average requirements and are therefore approximate.

TENSION

28 sts and 36 rows to 10cm square on 3.25mm needles (or size needed to obtain given tension).

ABBREVIATIONS

alt = alternate; **beg** = beginning; **cont** = continue; **dec** = decrease; **foll** = following; **inc** = increase; **K** = knit; **P** = purl; **patt** = pattern; **rem** = remaining; **rep** = repeat; **RS** = right side; **st(s)** = stitch(es); **st st** = stocking stitch; **tbl** = through back of loop; **tog** = together; **WS** = wrong side.

BACK

With 2.75mm needles and A, cast on 128(132:140:148:152) sts. Work in K2, P2 rib for 7cm.
Change to 3.25mm needles and starting with a K row, work in st st.
Cont straight until work measures 38(42:44: 46:47) cm from beg, ending with a P row.

Shape armholes

Dec 1 st at both ends on next 8 rows.
[112(116:124:132:136) sts.] *.
Work straight until armhole measures 24cm.

Shape shoulders

Cast off 7(7:7:8:8) sts at beg of next 8 rows, and 4(5:8:8:9) sts at beg of next 2 rows.
Leave rem 48(50:52:52:54) sts on a stitch holder.

FRONT

With 2.75mm needles and A, cast on 128(132:140:148:152) sts. Work in K2, P2 rib for 7cm. Change to 3.25mm needles and starting with a K row, work in st st.
Cont straight until work measures 11(15:18: 19:20)cm from beg, ending with a P row.
Next row: K32(34:38:42:44) sts, K 1st row from chart, K to end.
Next row: P29(31:35:39:41) sts, P 2nd row from chart, P to end.

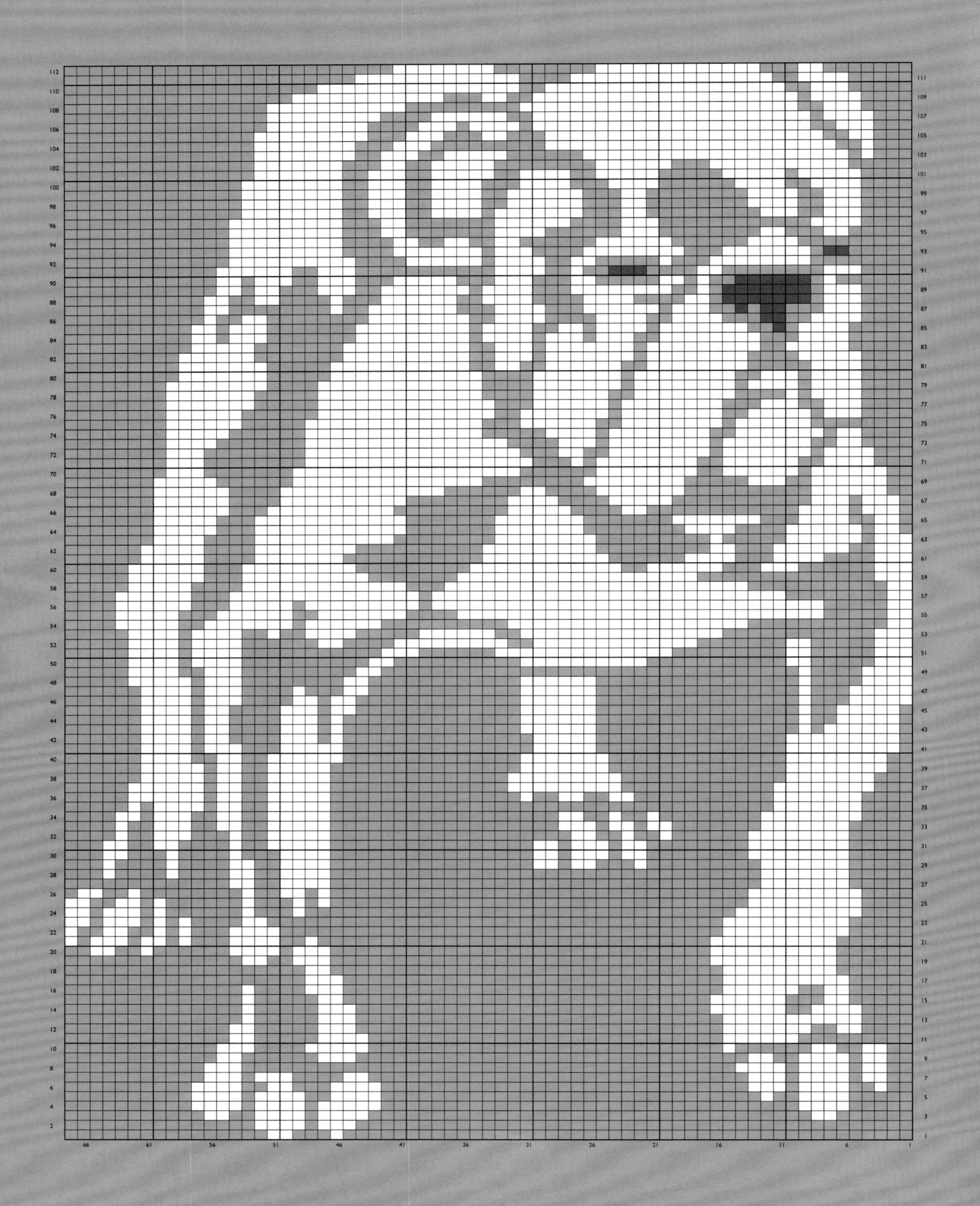

Cont working rows of patt from chart as placed.
At the same time: When work measures same as back to armholes, ending with a P row, shape armholes.

Shape armholes
Dec 1 st at both ends on next 8 rows [112(116:124:132:136) sts], keeping patt over sts as set.
Work straight until armhole measures 16cm.

Shape neck
With RS of work facing, K44(45:48:52:54) sts, turn, leave rem sts on a spare needle.
Dec 1 st at neck edge on next 12 rows.
Work straight until length measures same as back to shoulder, ending at armhole edge.

Shape shoulders
Cast off 7(7:7:8:8) sts at beg, next and foll 3 alt rows. Work 1 row. Cast off 4(5:8:8:9) sts.
With RS of work facing, slip next 24(26:28:28:30) sts onto a stitch holder.
Rejoin yarn to next st and K to end of row.
Complete to match first side from * to end.

SLEEVES (both alike)
With 2.75mm needles and A, cast on 68 sts.
Work in K2, P2 rib for 8cm.
Change to 3.25mm needles and starting with a K row, work in st st.
Inc 1 st at both ends of the 6th and every foll 4th row until there are 132 sts.
*** Work straight until sleeve measures 48cm from beg, ending with a P row.

A Grey

B White

C Black

Roddy Llewellyn, ace gardener, shows his bulldog spirit in 1986.

Shape armhole
Dec 1 st at both ends on next 8 rows. [116 sts.]
Cast off.

NECKBAND
Sew up left shoulder seam.
With 2.75mm needles and RS of work facing, pick up and knit 48(50:52:52:54) sts from back neck, 24 sts from left side neck, 24(26:28:28:30) sts from centre front, and 24 sts from right side neck. [120(124:128:128:132) sts.]
Work K2, P2 rib for 5cm. Cast off loosely in rib.

TO MAKE UP
Press work according to yarn instructions, omitting ribbing. Sew up right shoulder and neckband.
Fold neckband in half and sew down on wrong side.
Sew in sleeves. Sew up side and sleeve seams.

Wee scottie

This wee little doggie was originally modelled for us by the much loved and much missed actor Richard Briers. Doing the honours today is the lovely James Hattsmith, a very talented illustrator, compositor and VFX artist – and equally talented friend.

MEASUREMENTS

To fit chest/bust: 87(92:97:102:107)cm
Length: 61(65:67:69:71)cm
Sleeve length: 49(49:50:51:51)cm
Figures in brackets refer to the larger sizes.
Where only one figure is given this refers to all sizes.

MATERIALS

9(9:10:11:11) x 50g balls of 4-ply yarn in main shade – blue (A)
1 x 50g ball of 4-ply yarn in each of contrast shades – white (B) and cerise (C)
1 pair each of 2.75mm and 3.25mm knitting needles
The quantities of yarn given are based on average requirements and are therefore approximate.

TENSION

28 stitches and 36 rows to 10cm square over st st on 3.25mm needles (or size needed to obtain given tension).

ABBREVIATIONS

alt = alternate; **beg** = beginning; **cont** = continue; **dec** = decrease; **foll** = following; **inc** = increase; **K** = knit; **P** = purl; **patt** = pattern; **rem** = remaining; **rep** = repeat; **RS** = right side; **st(s)** = stitch(es); **st st** = stocking stitch; **tbl** = through back of loop; **tog** = together; **WS** = wrong side.

BACK

With 2.75mm needles and A, cast on 128(132:140:148:152) sts. Work in K2, P2 rib for 7cm.
Change to 3.25mm needles and, starting with a K row, work in st st.
Cont straight until work measures 42(46:48:49:51)cm from beg, ending with a P row.

Shape armholes

Inc 1 st at both ends of the next and every foll 10th row, 6 times. [142(146:154:162:166) sts.]
Work 5(7:7:9:9) rows straight.

Shape shoulders

Cast off 6(6:6:7:7) sts at beg of next 14 rows and 5(6:9:6:7) sts at beg of next 2 rows.
Leave rem 48(50:52:52:54) sts on a stitch holder.

FRONT

With 2.75mm needles and A, cast on 128(132:140:148:152) sts. Work in K2, P2 rib for 7cm.
Change to 3.25mm needles and starting with a K row, work in st st.
Cont straight until work measures 23(27:29:30:32)cm from beg, ending with a P row.
Next row: K20(22:26:30:32) sts, K 1st row of patt from chart, K to end of row.
Next row: P20(22:26:30:32) sts, P 2nd row of patt from chart, P to end of row.

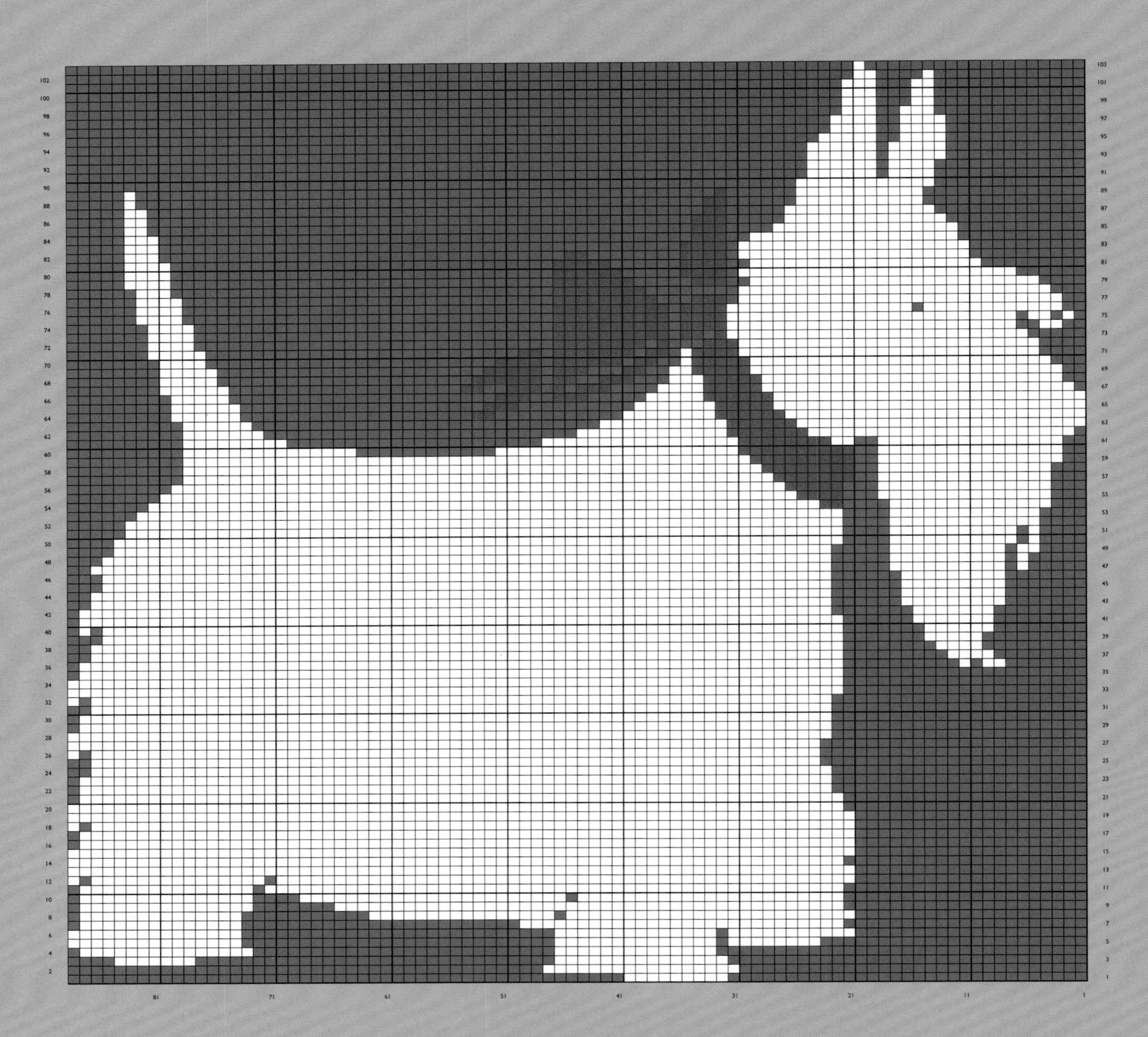

A Blue

B White

C Cerise

Cont working rows of patt from chart as placed.
At the same time: When work measures same as back to armholes, ending with a P row, shape armholes.

Shape armholes

Inc 1 st at both ends of next and every foll 10th row, 6 times.
At the same time: When work measures 56(60:62:64:66)cm from beg, shape neck.

Shape neck

With RS of work facing, K57(59:62:66:67) sts, turn, leave rem sts on a spare needle.
* Dec 1 st at neck edge on next 12 rows.
Work straight until length measures same as back to shoulder, ending at armhole edge.

Shape shoulders

Cast off 6(6:6:7:7) sts at beg of next and foll 6 alt rows.
Work 1 row.
Cast off 5(6:9:6:7) sts.
With RS of work facing, slip next 24(26:28:28:30) sts onto a stitch holder.
Rejoin yarn to next st and work to end of row.
[57(59:62:66:67) sts.]
Complete to match first side from * to end.

SLEEVES (both alike)

With 2.75mm needles and A, cast on 64(64:68:68:72) sts. Work in K2, P2 rib for 8cm.
On the last row inc 48(48:48:52:52) sts evenly.
[112(112:116:120:124) sts.]
Change to 3.25mm needles and starting with a K row, work in st st.
Cont straight until work measures 49(49:50:51:51) cm from beg.
Cast off.

NECKBAND

Sew up left shoulder seam.
With 2.75mm needles and A and RS of work facing, pick up and knit 48(50:52:52:54) sts from back neck, 24 sts from left side neck, 24(26:28:28:30) sts from centre front and 24 sts from right side neck. [120(124:128:128:132) sts.]
Work in K2, P2 rib for 5cm. Cast off loosely in rib.

TO MAKE UP

Press work according to yarn instructions, omitting ribbing. Sew up right shoulder and neckband. Fold neckband in half and sew down on WS. Sew in sleeves. Sew up side and sleeve seams

The delightful Richard Briers modelling our delightful Westie jumper in 1986.

What a hoot!

A wise old owl sat on an oak; the more he saw the less he spoke; the less he spoke the more he heard; why aren't we like that wise old bird? *So wrote Edward Hersey Richard, the second prime minister of Bermuda. Which is rather appropriate as the collective noun for owls is… a parliament. And 'whoo' is that tawny beauty in the jumper? It is actress, author, cake-maker and friend Jane Asher, who first modelled a Brandreth family wit-knit in the 1980s and is kindly doing us the honour all over again.*

MEASUREMENTS

To fit chest/bust: 81(86:91:97:102:107:112)cm
Length: 62(63:65:68:71:75:77)cm
Sleeve length: 42(44:46:48:50:52:52)cm
Figures in brackets refer to the larger sizes.
Where only one figure is given this refers to all sizes.

MATERIALS

6(7:7:8:8:9:9) x 50g balls of 4-ply yarn in main shade – burgundy (MC)
1 x 50g ball of 4-ply yarn in each of contrast shades – dark brown (A), light camel (B), cream (C)
Small amounts of 4-ply yarn in contrast shades – black (D) and gold (E)
1 pair each of 2.75mm and 3.25mm knitting needles
2 stitch holders
1 stitch marker
The quantities of yarn given are based on average requirements and are therefore approximate.

TENSION

28 stitches and 36 rows to 10cm square over st st on 3.25mm needles (or size needed to obtain given tension).

ABBREVIATIONS

alt = alternate; beg = beginning; cont = continue; dec = decrease; foll = following; inc = increase; K = knit; K2tog = knit 2 together; P = purl; P2tog = purl 2 together; patt = pattern; pm = place marker; psso = pass slipped stitch over; rem = remaining; rep = repeat; RS = right side; s = slip; st(s) = stitch(es); st st = stocking stitch; tbl = through back of loop; tog = together; WS = wrong side.

BACK

With 2.75mm needles and MC, use thumb method to cast on 127(135:143:151:159:169:177) sts.
Row 1 (RS): *K1, P1, rep from * to last st, K1.
Row 2: P1, *K1, P1, rep from * to end of row.
Work 20 more rows in K1, P1 rib.
Change to 3.25mm needles and proceed as follows:
Row 1: K.
Row 2: P.
Working in st st, cont until back measures 42(43:44:45:46:47:48)cm, ending with a WS row.

Shape armholes

Cast off 8 sts at beg next 2 rows.
[111(119:127:135:143:153:161) sts.]
Row 1: K1, s1, K1, psso, K to last 3 sts, K2tog, K1.
[109(117:125:133:141:151:159) sts.]
Row 2: P1, P2tog, P to last 3 sts, P2tog tbl, P1.
[107(115:123:131:139:149:157) sts.]
Rows 1 and 2 set dec for armholes.

Work 21 rows, dec 1 st as before at each end of next 7 rows, and then on every foll alt row. [79(87:95:103:111:121:129) sts.]
** Cont in st st without shaping until armhole measures 14(15:16:18:20:22:24)cm, ending with WS row.

Shape back neck

Row 1: K17(21:24:28:30:35:38) sts, turn, leave rem 62(66:71:75:81:86:91) sts on a stitch holder. Working on these 17(21:24:28:30:35:38) sts only proceed as follows:
Next row: Dec 1 st at neck edge and P to end with RS facing for next row. [16(20:23:27:29:34:37) sts.]

Shape shoulder

Cast off 4(5:7:8:9:10:11) sts at beg of next and foll alt row.
At the same time: Dec 1 st at neck edge of next 3 rows. [5(7:6:8:8:11:12) sts.]
Work 1 row. Cast off rem 5(7:6:8:8:11:12) sts.
With RS facing, slip centre 45(45:47:47:51:51:53) sts onto a stitch holder. Rejoin yarn to rem 17(21:24:28:30:35:38) sts and proceed as follows:
Next row: Dec 1 st at neck edge, K to end of row with WS facing for next row. [16(20:23:27:29:34:37) sts.]
Cast off 4(5:7:8:9:10:11) sts at beg of next and foll alt row.
At the same time: Dec 1 st at neck edge of next 3 rows. [5(7:6:8:8:12:13) sts.]
Work 1 row. Cast off rem 5(7:6:8:8:12:13) sts.

PLACEMENT OF CHART

Follow patt for front as opposite until work measures 11(13:15:18:21:24:29)cm, ending with a WS row.

Next row: Starting at the point indicated for the size you are knitting, K across 102(106:110:114:118:123:127) sts of chart, pm, K across rem 25(29:33:37:41:46:50) sts of row in MC. This row shows placement of chart. Complete 110 rows of chart.
At the same time: Cont working front patt shapings.

FRONT

Work as given for Back to **.
Cont in st st without shaping until armhole measures 9(10:11:13:15:17:18.5)cm, ending with WS row.

Shape front neck

Next row: K27(31:34:38:42:45:49), turn, leave rem 52(56:61:65:69:76:80) sts on a stitch holder.
Working on these 27(31:34:38:42:45:49) sts only, proceed as follows:
Work 18 rows dec 1 st at neck edge of next 10 rows, then on 4 foll alt rows. [13(17:20:24:28:31:35) sts.]
Work 1 row with RS facing for next row.
Cast off 4(5:6:8:9:10:11) sts at beg of next and foll alt row. [5(7:8:8:10:11:13) sts.]
Work 1 row. Cast off rem 5(7:8:8:10:11:13) sts.
With RS facing, slip centre 25(25:27:27:27:31:31) sts onto a stitch holder. Rejoin yarn to rem 27(31:34:38:42:45:49) sts, and proceed as follows:
Work 18 rows dec 1 st at neck edge of next 10 rows, then on 4 foll alt rows. [13(17:20:24:28:31:35) sts.]
Work 1 row with WS facing for next row. Cast off 4(5:6:8:9:10:11) sts at beg of next and foll alt row. [5(7:8:8:10:11:13) sts.]
Work 1 row. Cast off rem 5(7:8:8:10:11:13) sts.

SLEEVES (both alike)

With 2.75mm needles and MC, cast on 63(65:67:69:73:75:79) sts, work 22 rows in K1, P1 rib.
Change to 3.25mm needles and working in st st, inc 1 st at each end of 3rd and every foll 4th row to 101(105:109:105:97:95:99) sts, then for every foll 0(0:0:6th:6th:6th:6th) row until 0(0:0:113:117:121:125) sts.
Cont without shaping until sleeve measures 37(39:41:45:49:52:52)cm, or length required, ending with a WS row.

Shape top

Cast off 8 sts at beg next 2 rows. [85(89:93:97:101:105:109) sts.]
Dec 1 st as before on each end of next 3 rows, then on every foll alt row to 73 sts, then on foll 13 rows, ending with RS facing for next row. [47 sts.]
Cast off 5 sts at beg of next 4 rows. Cast off rem 27 sts.

NECKBAND

Join right shoulder seam.
With RS facing, using 2.75mm needles and MC, pick up and knit 16(18:18:20:20:20:21) sts evenly along left side of front neck, knit across 25(25:27:27:27:31:31) sts left on stitch holder at front of neck, pick up and knit 16(18:18:20:20:20:21) sts evenly along right side of front neck, pick up and knit 6 sts evenly along right side of back neck, knit across 45(45:47:47:51:51:53) sts left on stitch holder at back of neck, pick up and knit 6 sts evenly along left side of front neck. [114(118:122:126:130:134:138) sts.]
Work 11 rows in K1, P1 rib. Cast off in rib.

TO MAKE UP

Using contrast E, embroider eye details on the owl as shown in chart. Join left shoulder and neckband seams. Sew in sleeves. Join side and sleeve seams. Weave in all ends. Pin out garment to measurements given. Cover with damp cloths and leave until dry. See ball band for washing and further care instructions.

Bananarama

The banana lays claim to be the world's most popular fruit and this fresh and fruity jumper certainly has universal 'ap-peel'. Adapted from an original George Hostler design, it's sweet and simple – just like our model Mark Evans.

MEASUREMENTS

To fit chest/bust: 87(92:97:102:107)cm
Length: 61(65:67:69:71)cm
Sleeve length: 49(49:50:51:51)cm
Figures in brackets refer to the larger sizes.
Where only one figure is given this refers to all sizes.

MATERIALS

11(11:12:14:14) x 50g balls of 4-ply yarn in main shade – green (A)
1 x 50g ball of 4-ply yarn in each of contrast shades – yellow (B), cream (C) and white (D)
1 pair each of 2.75mm and 3.25mm knitting needles
The quantities of yarn given are based on average requirements and are therefore approximate.

TENSION

28 stitches and 36 rows to 10cm square over st st on 3.25mm needles (or size needed to obtain given tension).

ABBREVIATIONS

alt = alternate; beg = beginning; cont = continue; dec = decrease; foll = following; inc = increase; K = knit; P = purl; patt = pattern; rem = remaining; rep = repeat; RS = right side; st(s) = stitch(es); st st = stocking stitch; tbl = through back of loop; tog = together; WS = wrong side.

BACK

With 2.75mm needles and A, cast on 128(132:140:148:152) sts. Work in K1, P1 rib for 5cm.
Change to 3.25mm needles and starting with a K row, work in st st.
Cont straight until work measures 42(46:48:49:51) cm from beg, ending with a P row.

Shape armholes

* Inc 1 st at both ends of the next and every foll 10th row, 6 times *. [142(146:154:162:166) sts.]
Work 5(7:7:9:9) rows straight.

Shape shoulders

Cast off 6(6:6:7:7) sts at beg of next 14 rows, and 5(6:9:6:7) sts at beg next 2 rows. Leave rem 48(50:52:52:54) sts on a holder.

FRONT

Work as given for back until work measures 25(29:31:33:35)cm from beg, ending with a P row.
Next row: K36(38:42:46:48) sts, K the 1st row of patt from chart, K to end.
Next row: P37(39:43:47:49) sts, P the 2nd row of patt from chart, P to end.
Cont working rows of patt from chart as placed.
At the same time: When work measures same as back to armholes, ending with a P row, shape armholes.

Shape armholes

Work as back from * to *.

At the same time: When work measures 56(60:62:64:66)cm from beg, shape neck.

Shape neck

With RS of work facing, K57(59:62:66:67) sts, turn, leave rem sts on a spare needle.

** Dec 1 st at neck edge on the next 12 rows.

Work straight until length measures same as back to shoulder, ending at armhole edge.

Shape shoulders

Cast off 6(6:6:7:7) sts at beg of next and foll 6 alt rows. Work 1 row.

Cast off 5(6:9:6:7) sts.

With RS of work facing, slip next 24(26:28:28:30) sts onto a stitch holder.

Rejoin yarn to next st and K to end of row.

Complete to match first side from ** to end.

SLEEVES (both alike)

With 3.75mm needles and A, cast on 64(64:68:68:72) sts. Work in K1, P1 rib for 5cm.

On the last row, inc 48(48:48:52:52) sts evenly. [112(112:116:120:120) sts.]

Change to 3.25mm needles and starting with a K row, work in st st.

Cont straight until work measures 49(49:50:51:51)cm from beg.

Cast off.

NECKBAND

Sew up left shoulder seam.

With 2.75mm needles and A and RS of work facing, pick up and knit 48(50:52:52:54) sts from back neck, 24 sts from left side neck, 24(26:28:28:30) sts from centre front, and 24 sts from right side neck. [120(124:128:128:132) sts.]

Work in K1, P1 rib for 5cm.

Cast off loosely in rib.

TO MAKE UP

Press work according to yarn instructions, omitting ribbing. Sew up right shoulder and neckband. Fold neckband in half and sew down on WS. Sew in sleeves. Sew up side and sleeve seams.

A Green
B Yellow
C Cream
D White

Strawberry delight

The gorgeous Emma McQuiston is the Viscountess of Weymouth. She is also a fabulous chef who is passionate about creating healthy, delicious food which is as good for you as it tastes. Which makes sense, as Emma herself is as lovely on the inside as she is on the outside. Here she is looking sweet and summery in our strawberry knit, an organic version of George Hostler's eighties original.

MEASUREMENTS

To fit chest/bust: 87(92:97:102:107)cm
Length: 61(65:67:69:71)cm
Sleeve length: 49(49:50:51:51)cm
Figures in brackets refer to the larger sizes.
Where only one figure is given this refers to all sizes.

MATERIALS

9(9:10:11:11) x 50g balls of 4-ply yarn in main shade – cream (A)
2 x 50g balls of 4-ply yarn in contrast shade – red (B)
Small amounts of contrast shades – green (C) and yellow (D)
1 pair each of 2.75mm and 3.25mm knitting needles
The quantities of yarn given are based on average requirements and are therefore approximate.

TENSION

28 stitches and 36 rows to 10cm square over st st on 3.25mm needles (or size needed to obtain given tension).

ABBREVIATIONS

alt = alternate; **beg** = beginning; **cont** = continue; **dec** = decrease; **foll** = following; **inc** = increase; **K** = knit; **P** = purl; **patt** = pattern; **rem** = remaining **rep** = repeat; **RS** = right side; **st(s)** = stitch(es); **st st** = stocking stitch; **tog** = together; **WS** = wrong side.

BACK

With 2.75mm needles and A, cast on 128(132:140:148:152) sts. Work in K2, P2 rib for 7cm.
Change to 3.25mm needles, and starting with a K row, work in st st.
Cont straight until work measures 42(46:48:49:51) cm from beg ending with a P row.

Shape armholes

Inc 1 st at both ends of the next and every foll 10th row, 6 times.
Cont until there are 142(146:154:162:166) sts.
Work 5(7:7:9:9) rows straight.

Shape shoulders

Cast off 6(6:6:7:7) sts at beg of next 14 rows, and 5(6:9:6:7) sts at beg of next 2 rows.
Leave rem 48(50:52:52:54) sts on a holder.

FRONT

Work as given for back until work measures 22(26:28:30:32)cm from beg, ending with a p row.
Next row: K44(46:50:54:56) sts, K the 1st row of the patt from chart, K to end of row.
Next row: P44(46:50:54:56) sts, P the 2nd row of the patt from chart, P to end of row.
Cont working rows of patt from chart as placed.

At the same time: When work measures same as back to armholes, ending with a P row, shape armholes.

Shape armholes

Inc 1 st at both ends of the next and every foll 10th row, 6 times.
At the same time: When the patt rows from the chart have been worked cont in A only until work measures 56(60:62:64:66)cm from beg.

Shape neck

With RS of work facing, K57(59:62:66:67) sts, turn, leave rem sts on a spare needle.
* Dec 1 st at neck edge on the next 12 rows.
Work straight until length measures same as back to shoulder, ending at armhole edge.

Shape shoulders

Cast off 6(6:6:7:7) sts at beg of next and foll 6 alt rows. Work 1 row.
Cast off 5(6:9:6:7) sts.
With RS of work facing, slip the next 24(26:28:28:30) sts onto a stitch holder.
Rejoin yarn to next st and K to end of row.
Complete to match side from * to end.

SLEEVES (both alike)

With 2.75mm needles and MC, cast on 64(64:68:68:72) sts.
Work in K2, P2 rib for 7cm.
On the last row inc 48 sts evenly.
[112(112:116:116:120) sts].
Change to 3.25mm needles and, starting with a K row, work in st st.
Cont straight until work measures 49(49:50:51:51) cm from beg.
Cast off.

NECKBAND

Sew up left shoulder seam. With 2.75mm needles and RS of work facing, pick up and knit 48(50:52:52:54) sts from back neck, 24 sts from left side neck, 24(26:28:28:30) sts from centre front and 24 sts from right side neck.
[120(124:128:128:132) sts.]
Work in K2, P2 rib for 5cm. Cast off loosely in rib.

TO MAKE UP

Press work according to yarn instructions, omitting ribbing. Sew up right shoulder and neckband.
Fold neckband in half and sew down on wrong side.
Sew in sleeves. Sew up side and sleeve seams.

A Cream

B Red

C Green

D Yellow

lambretta

Boiled egg

Peter Ginn is an archeologist and television presenter who has collected many an egg whilst recreating farm life in the Victorian, Edwardian and Tudor eras for his popular series on BBC2. He's also milked goats, trained carthorses, corralled grouchy geese, and even played midwife to a litter of piglets... no yoke!

MEASUREMENTS

To fit chest/bust: 87(92:97:102:107)cm
Length: 57(58.5:61:63.5:66)cm
Sleeve length: 48.5(49.5:51:52:53.5)cm
Figures in brackets refer to the larger sizes.
Where only one figure is given this refers to all sizes.

MATERIALS

9(10:11:11:12) x 50g balls of 4-ply yarn in main shade – dark blue (A)
1 x 50g ball of 4-ply yarn in each of contrast shades – white (B), red (C), cream (D), light blue (E)
Small amount of contrast shade – yellow (F)
1 pair each of 2.75mm and 3mm knitting needles
The quantities of yarn given are based on average requirements and are therefore approximate.

TENSION

32 stitches and 40 rows to 10cm square over st st on 3mm needles (or size needed to obtain given tension).

ABBREVIATIONS

alt = alternate; **beg** = beginning; **cont** = continue; **dec** = decrease; **foll** = following; **inc** = increase; **K** = knit; **P** = purl; **patt** = pattern; **rem** = remaining **rep** = repeat; **RS** = right side; **st(s)** = stitch(es); **st st** = stocking stitch; **tog** = together; **WS** = wrong side.

FRONT

With 2.75mm needles and A, cast on 126(134:142:150:158) sts.
Work in K2, P2 rib for 4 cm.
Change to 3mm needles.
Inc row: K, inc 20 sts evenly across row. [146(154:162:170: 178) sts.]
Next row: P.
Cont straight in st st until work measures 20(20.5:21.5:23:24)cm from cast-on edge , ending on a WS row.

Place Chart 1

Change to C and K58(62:66:70:74) sts, work 1st row of Chart 1, K to end of row.
Next row: P58(62:66:70:74) sts, work 2nd row of Chart 1, P to end of row.
Work chart as now set (changing back to A for stitches outside the chart at row 5).
Cont straight in st st until work measures 48.5(50:52.5:55:57.5)cm, ending on a WS row.

Shape neck

Next row: K57(61:65:69:73) sts, put rem sts onto a stitch holder.
Next row: Cast off 3 sts, P to end.
Next row: K.
Rep last two rows one more time.
Next row: Cast off 2 sts, P to end.
Next row: K.
Rep last two rows two more times.

CHART 1

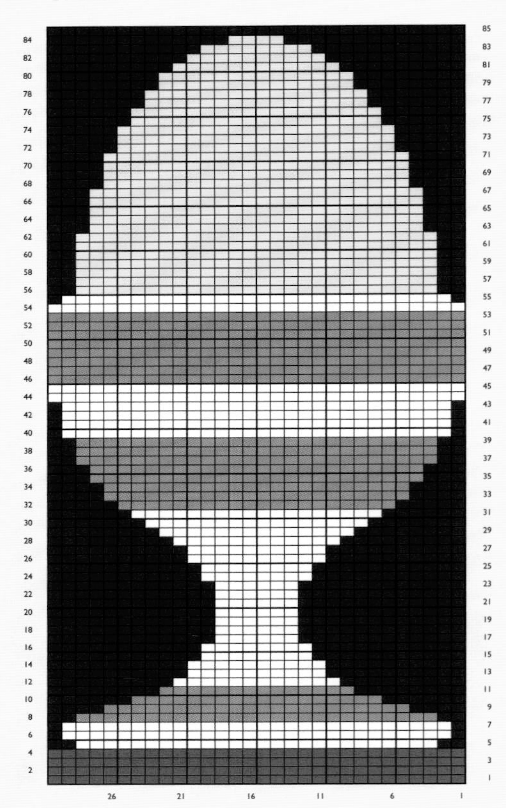

CHART 2

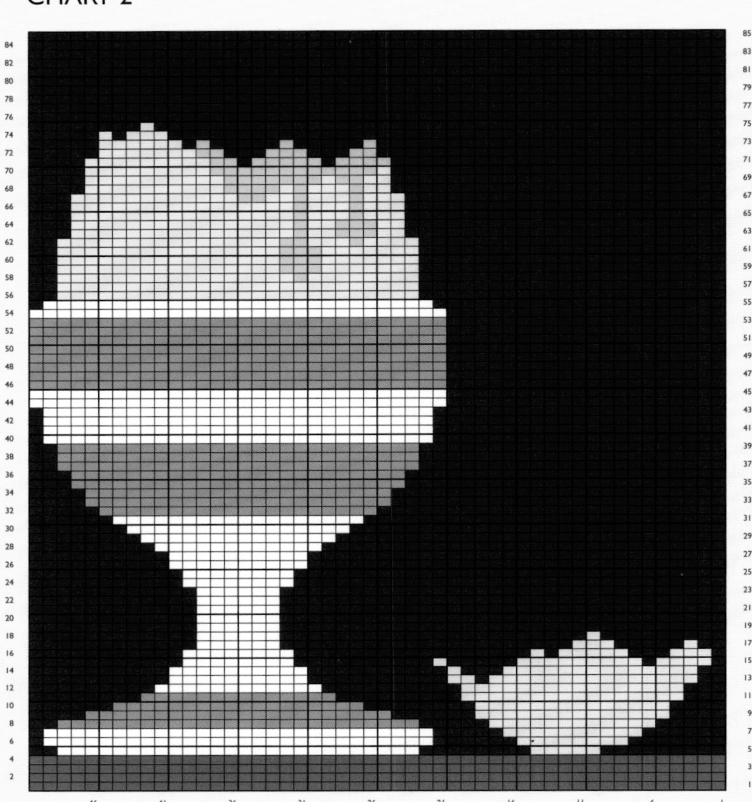

CHART 3

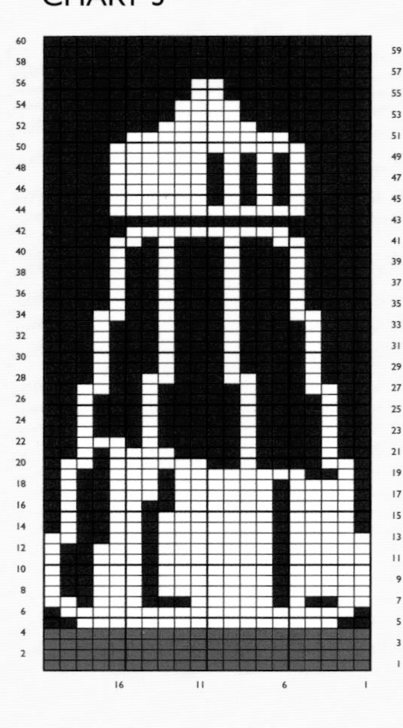

- **A** Dark blue
- **B** White
- **C** Red
- **D** Cream
- **E** Light blue
- **F** Yellow

Dec at neck edge on each WS row 3 times.
[42(46:50:54:58) sts.]
Work 14 rows in st st.
Cast off loosely.
Return to rem stitches and slip first 32 sts onto a stitch holder.
With RS facing, rejoin yarn and K to end.
[57(61:65:69:73) sts.]
Next row: P.

Next row: Cast off 3 sts, K to end.
Next row: P.
Rep last two rows one more time.
Next row: Cast off 2 sts, K to end.
Next row: P.
Rep last two rows two more times.
Dec at neck edge on every RS row 3 times.
[42(46:50:54:58) sts.]
Work 13 rows in st st.
Cast off loosely.

BACK

With 2.75mm needles and A, cast on 126(134:142:150:158) sts.
Work in K2, P2 rib for 4 cm.
Change to 3mm needles.
Inc row: K, inc 20 sts evenly across row.
[146(154:162:170: 178) sts.]
Next row: P.
Cont straight in st st until work measures 20(20.5:21.5:23:24)cm, from cast-on edge, ending on a WS row.

Place Chart 2

Change to C and K38(42:46:50:54) sts, work 1st row of Chart 2, K to end.
Next row: P58(62:66:70:74) sts, work 2nd row of Chart 2, P to end.
Work chart as now set (changing back to A for stitches outside the chart at row 5).
Cont straight in st st until work measures 57(58.5:61:63.5:66)cm, ending on a WS row.

Shape shoulder

Cast off 42(46:50:54:58) sts loosely for shoulder, knit until there are 62 sts on right needle and slip onto a stitch holder.
Cast off rem 42(46:50:54:58) sts for shoulder.

RIGHT SLEEVE

With 2.75mm needles and A, cast on 72 sts.
Work in K2, P2 rib for 4 cm.
Change to 3mm needles.
Inc row: K, inc 20 sts evenly across row. [92 sts.]
Working in st st, inc 1 st at each end of foll 6th(6th:5th:5th:4th) rows until there are 128(134:142:148:156) sts.
At the same time: When work measures 31.5(32.5:34:35:36.5)cm, ending with a WS row, change to C and place Chart 3 in centre of sleeve.
Cont to inc outside chart as necessary and change back to A for stitches outside chart at row 5.
Work straight until work measures 48.5(49.5:51:52:53.5)cm.
Cast off loosely.

LEFT SLEEVE

Work as right sleeve, changing to C for 4 rows of st st where indicated but omitting chart.

NECKBAND

Join right shoulder seam.
With 2.75mm needles and A, pick up and knit 29 sts from left front neck, knit 32 sts from stitch holder, pick up and knit 29 sts up right neck edge and knit 62 sts from back neck stitch holder. [152 sts]
Work in K2, P2 rib for 6cm.
Cast off loosely.

TO MAKE UP

Join left shoulder and neckband.
Fold neckband in half and loosely slip stitch to the inside.
Measure and mark 23(24:25.5:26.5:28)cm each side of shoulder seam and sew sleeves between these marks.
Join side and sleeve seams.

Cherry on top

'Life is like a bowl of cherries. Don't take it serious. Life is too mysterious...'
So sang Ethel Merman, Rudy Valle and latterly Doris Day in the popular song of the same title from the 1930s. We think this cherry jumper is as cute and charming (and delightfully piquant) as the delicious Miss Asher who is modelling it for us here.

MEASUREMENTS

To fit chest/bust: 81(86:91:97:102:107:112)cm
Length: 62(63.5:65.5:67:69:70.5:72.5)cm
Sleeve length: 46(46:46:46:47:47:48)cm
Figures in brackets refer to the larger sizes.
Where only one figure is given this refers to all sizes.

MATERIALS

6(6:7:7:8:8:9) x 50g balls of DK yarn in main shade – light navy (MC)
1 x 50g ball of DK yarn in contrast shade – red (A)
Small amounts in contrast shades – cream (B), dark green (C) and green (D)
1 pair each of 3.25mm and 4mm knitting needles
4 stitch holders
2 stitch markers
The quantities of yarn given are based on average requirements and are therefore approximate.

TENSION

22 stitches and 28 rows to 10cm square over st st on 4mm needles (or size needed to obtain given tension).

ABBREVIATIONS

alt = alternate; **beg** = beginning; **cont** = continue; **dec** = decrease; **foll** = following; **inc** = increase; **K** = knit; **K2tog** = knit 2 together; **P** = purl; **P2tog** = purl 2 together; **patt** = pattern; **pm** = place marker; psso = pass slipped stitch over; **rem** = remaining **rep** = repeat; **RS** = right side; **s** = slip; **st(s)** = stitch(es); **st st** = stocking stitch; **tbl** = through back of loop; **tog** = together; **WS** = wrong side.

BACK

With 3.25mm needles and MC, use thumb method to cast on 106(112:122:134:142:150:156) sts.
Row 1: *K2, P2, rep from * to last 2 sts, K2.
Row 2: P2, *K2, P2, rep from * to end.
Work 11 more rows in K2, P2 rib.
Row 14: P7(10:11:7:7:5:8), P2tog, (P11 [11:7:5:4:4:4], P2tog) 7[7:11:17:21:23:23] times, P6[9:10:6:7:5:8]. 98[104:110:116:120:126:132] sts.
Change to 4mm needles and proceed as follows:
Row 1: K.
Row 2: P.
Continue to work in st st until back measures 40(41:42:43:44:45:46)cm, ending with a WS row.

Shape raglan

Cast off 4(5:5:6:7:8:8) sts at beg of next 2 rows. [90(94:100:104:106:110:116) sts.]
Row 1: K1, s1, K1, psso, K to last 3 sts, K2tog, K1. [88(92:98:102:104:108:114) sts.]
Row 2: P1, P2tog, P to last 3 sts, P2tog tbl, P1. [86(90:96:100:102:106:112) sts.]
Rows 1 and 2 set raglan shapings.
Work 0(0:4:4:4:6:8) rows dec 1 st as before at each

end of every row. [86(90:88:92:94:94:96) sts.] **
Proceed as follows:
Row 1: K1, s1, K1, psso, K to last 3 sts, K2tog, K1. [84(88:86:90:92:92:94) sts.]
Row 2: P.
Rows 1 and 2 set raglan shapings.
Work 46(48:48:50:52:52:54) rows dec 1 st as before at each end of next and every foll alt row. [38(40:40:42:42:42:44) sts.]
Leave rem 38(40:40:42:42:42:44) sts on a stitch holder.

PLACEMENT OF CHART
Follow patt for front as below until work measures 28(30:33:35:36:38:40)cm ending with a WS row.
Next row: K21(24:27:30:32:35:38) sts in MC, pm, knit across 46 sts of Row 1 of chart using intarsia method to change colour as required, pm, knit across rem of row in MC. This row shows placement of chart.
Complete 48 rows of chart.
At the same time: Cont working front patt shapings.

FRONT
Work as given for Back to **. Work 34(36:34:36:38:38:38) rows dec 1 st as before at each end of next and every foll alt row. [52(54:54:56:56:56:58) sts.]

Shape neck
Next row: K1, s1, K1, psso, K14, turn, leave rem 35(37:37:39:39:39:41) sts on a stitch holder.
Working on these 16 sts only, proceed as follows for all sizes:
Next row: P.
Next row: K1, s1, K1, psso, K to last 2 sts, K2tog. [14 sts.]
Next row: P2tog, P to end. [13 sts.]
Work 4 rows, dec 1 st as before at raglan edge in next and foll 2nd row.
At the same time: Dec 1 st at neck edge in every row. [7 sts.]
Work 4 rows, dec 1 st as before at each end of next and every foll alt row. [3 sts.]
Next row: K1, s1, K1, psso. [2 sts.]
Next row: P2tog.
Fasten off. With RS facing, working on rem 35(37:37:39:39:39:41) sts, slip 18(20:20:22:22:22:24) sts onto a stitch holder, rejoin yarn to rem 17 sts and K to last 3 sts, K2tog, K1. [16 sts.]
Next row: P.
Next row: K2tog, K to last 2 sts, K2tog, K1. [14 sts.]
Next row: P to last 2 sts, P2tog. [13 sts.]
Work 4 rows, dec 1 st at neck edge in every row.
At the same time: Dec 1 st as before at raglan edge in next and every foll 2nd row. [7 sts.]
Work 4 rows, dec 1 st as before at each end of next and every foll alt row. [3 sts.]
Next row: K1, K2tog. [2 sts.]
Next row: P2tog. Fasten off.

SLEEVES (both alike)
With 3.25mm needles and MC, use thumb method to cast on 58(58:60:60:62:62:64) sts. Work 13 rows in K2, P2 rib.
Row 14: P5(5:2:2:3:3:4), P2tog, (P3(3:4:4:4:4:4), P2tog) 9 times, P6(6:2:2:3:3:4). [48(48:50:50:52:52:54) sts.]
Change to 4mm needles and working in st st (throughout) inc 1 st at each end of 5th(5th:3rd:3rd:5th:3rd:3rd) and every foll 8th(8th:8th:6th:6th:6th:6th) row to 62(70:70:60:72:86:86) sts. Inc 1 st at each end of every foll 10th(10th:10th:8th:8th:8th:8th) row to 72(74:76:80:84:88:90) sts. Cont without

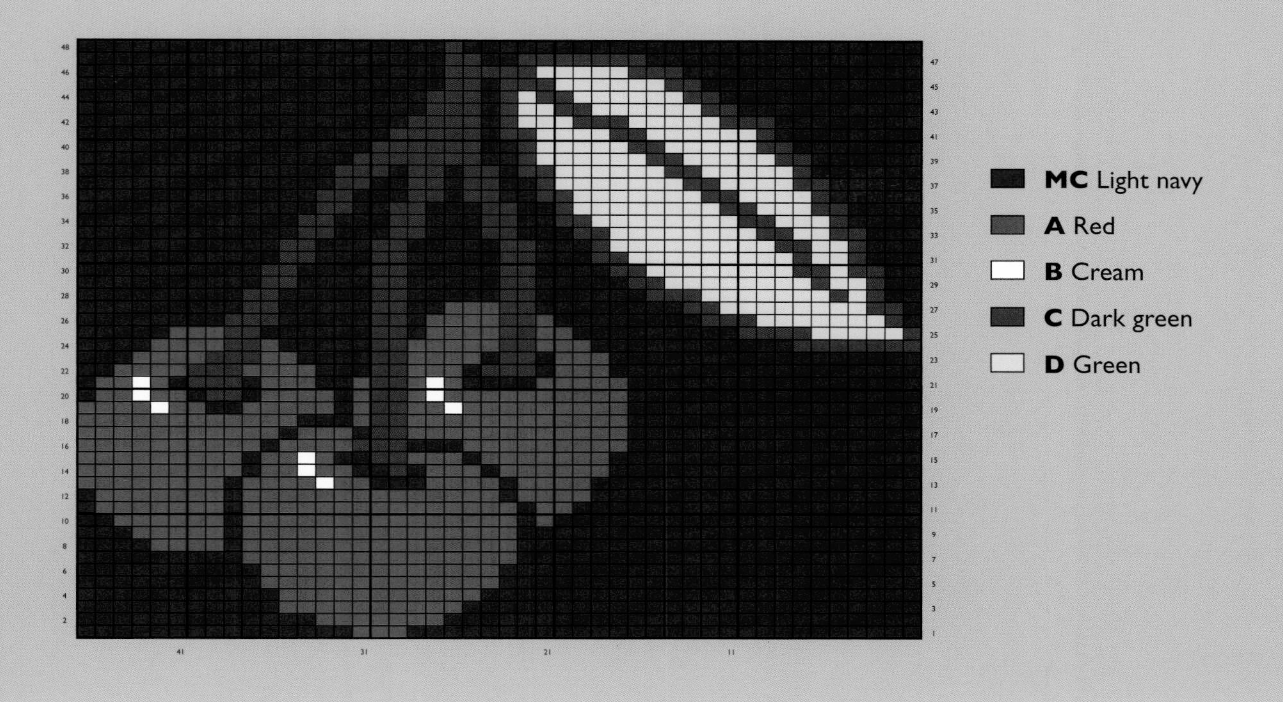

shaping until sleeve measures 46(46:46:46:47:47:48) cm or length required, ending with WS row.

Shape raglan

Cast off 4(5:5:6:7:8:8) sts at beg of next 2 rows. [64(64:66:68:70:72:74) sts.]

Row 1: K1, s1, K1, psso, K to last 3 sts, K2tog, K1. [62(62:64:66:68:70:72) sts.]

Row 2: P.

Rows 1 and 2 set raglan shapings. Work 8(10:14:14:14:18:18) rows, dec 1 st as before at each end of 3rd and every foll 4th row. [58(58:58:60:62:62:64) sts.]

Work 40(40:38:40:42:40:42) rows, dec 1 st as before at each end of next and every foll alt row. [18(18:20:20:20:22:22) sts.]

Leave rem 18(18:20:20:20:22:22) sts on a stitch holder.

NECKBAND

Join raglan seams leaving left back raglan open. With RS facing, using MC and 3.25mm needles, work across 18(18:20:20:20:22:22) sts left on stitch holder at top of left sleeve as follows: K8(8:9:9:9:10:10), K2tog, K8(8:9:9:9:10:10), pick up and knit 15 sts evenly along left side of neck, work across 18(20:20:22:22:22:24) sts left on stitch holder at front of neck as follows: K3(4:4:5:5:5:6), K2tog, K8, K2tog, K3(4:4:5:5:5:6), pick up and knit 15 sts evenly along right side of neck, work across 18(18:20:20:20:22:22) sts left on stitch holder at top of right sleeve as follows: K8(8:9:9:9:10:10), K2tog, K8(8:9:9:9:10:10), and work across 38(40:40:42:42:42:44) sts left on stitch holder at back of neck as follows: K6(7:7:8:8:8:9) K2tog, (K6, K2tog) 3 times, K6(7:7:8:8:8:9). [114(118:122:126:126:130:134) sts.]

Starting with 2nd row of K2, P2 rib, work 9 rows. Cast off in rib.

TO MAKE UP

Join left back raglan and neckband seams. Join side and sleeve seams. Weave in all ends. Pin out garment to the measurements given. Cover with damp cloths and leave until dry. See ball band for washing and further care instructions.

Beetle drive

We've all got the love bug for Hugh Bonneville in this VW inspired knit. Hugh is an acclaimed television, stage and screen actor. He gets rave reviews playing the Earl of Grantham, Lord Robert Crawley, in the global sensation Downtown Abbey, *a part that writer Julian Fellowes says he wrote specifically with him in mind. The beetle is a classic that will never go out of style, just like Hugh – and this jumper.*

MEASUREMENTS

To fit chest/bust: 87(92:97:102:107:112)cm
Length: 64(66:69:72:74:77)cm
Sleeve length: 47(47:48:48:49:49)cm

MATERIALS

11(12:12:13:14:15) x 50g balls of DK yarn in main shade – blue (MC)
1 x 50g ball of DK yarn in contrast shade – red (A).
Small amounts of contrast shades – dark grey (B), silver (C) and white (D)
1 pair each of 3.75mm and 4mm knitting needles
The quantities of yarn given are based on average requirements and are therefore approximate.

TENSION

22 stitches and 28 rows to 10cm square over st st on 4mm needles (or size needed to obtain given tension).

ABBREVIATIONS

alt = alternate; **beg** = beginning; **cont** = continue; **dec** = decrease; **foll** = following; **inc** = increase; **K** = knit; **P** = purl; **patt** = pattern; **rem** = remaining; **rep** = repeat; **RS** = right side; **st(s)** = stitch(es); **st st** = stocking stitch; **tbl** = through back of loop; **tog** = together; **WS** = wrong side.

BACK

With 3.75 mm needles and MC, cast on 108(114:120:126:130:138) sts.
Working in K2, P2 rib, work 2 rows MC, 2 rows A, then 5cm in MC.
Change to 4mm needles and starting with a K row, work in st st. Cont straight until work measures 34 (36:38:41:43:46)cm from beg, ending with a P row.

Shape armholes

* Dec 1 st at both ends on next and foll 6 alt rows. [94(100:106:112:116:124) sts.]
* Work straight until armhole measures 26(26:27:27:28:28)cm.

Shape shoulders

Cast off 6(6:6:7:7:7) sts at beg of next 8 rows, and 2(4:6:4:5:8) sts at beg of next 2 rows.
Leave rem 42(44:46:48:50:52) sts on a holder.

FRONT

Work as given for back until work measures 12(14:16:19:22:24)cm, ending with a P row.
Next row: K4(7:10:13:15:19) sts, K 1st row of patt from chart, K to end of row.
Next row: P5(8:11:14:16:20) sts, P 2nd row of patt from chart, P to end of row.
Cont working rows of patt from chart as placed.
When work measures same as back to armholes, shape armholes.

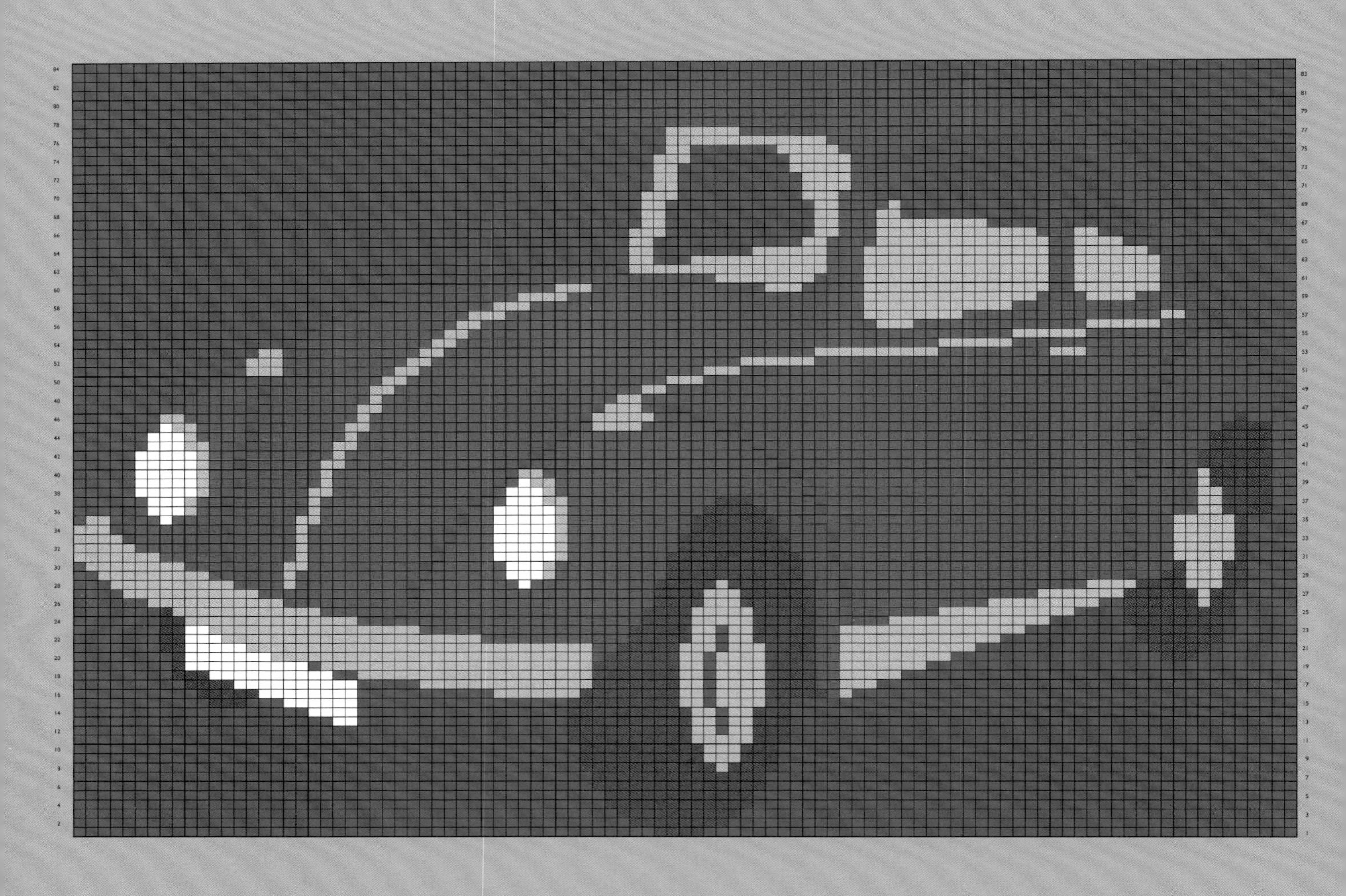

A Blue
B Red
C Dark grey
D Silver
E White

Shape armholes

Work as given for back from * to *, keeping patt over central sts as set.
Work straight until armhole measures 20.5cm.

Shape neck

With RS of work facing, K37(39:42:44:45:48) sts, turn, leave rem sts on a spare needle.
** Dec 1 st at neck edge on the next 12 rows.
Work straight until length measures same as back to shoulder ending at armhole edge.

Shape shoulders

Cast off 5(6:6:7:7:7) sts at beg of next and foll 3 alt rows.
Work 1 row. Cast off 5(3:6:4:5:8) sts.
With RS of work facing, slip next 20(22:22:24:26:28) sts onto a stitch holder.
Rejoin yarn to next st and K to end of row.
Complete to match first side from ** to end.

SLEEVES (both alike)

With 3.75mm needles and MC, cast on 62(62:64:64:68:68) sts.
Working in K2, P2 rib, work 2 rows in MC, 2 rows in A, then 5cm in MC.
Change to 4mm needles and starting with a K row, work in st st.
Inc 1 st at both ends on the next and every foll 4th row until there are 114(114:122:122:130:130) sts.
Work straight until sleeve measures 47(47:48:48:49:49)cm from beg, ending with a P row.

Shape top

Dec 1 st at both ends on next and foll 6 alt rows.
[108 sts].
Work 1 row. Cast off.

NECKBAND

Sew up left shoulder seam.
With 3.75mm needles and MC, pick up and knit 42(44:46:48:50:52) sts from back neck, 24 sts from left side neck, 20(22:22:24:26:28) sts from centre front and 24 sts from right side neck.
[110(114:116:120:124:128) sts].
Working in K2, P2 rib, work 5 rows in MC, 2 rows in A, 2 rows MC.
Cast off loosely in rib.

TO MAKE UP

Press work according to yarn instructions omitting ribbing. Sew up right shoulder and neckband. Mark 26(26:27:27:28:28)cm down from shoulders for armholes. Sew in sleeves between marks. Sew up side and sleeve seams.

Pole position

Fast track your way to pole position in our racy Formula One jumper, winningly modelled here by Jake Spark. Sparky by name, sparky by nature – and a first to cousin to Saethryd and a nephew by marriage to Gyles. (Knitting is a game the whole family can play.)

MEASUREMENTS

To fit chest/bust: 87(92:97:102:107)cm
Length: 57(60:65:69:73)cm
Sleeve length: 46(48:48:48:50)cm
Figures in brackets refer to the larger sizes.
Where only one figure is given this refers to all sizes.

MATERIALS

5(5:6:6:7) x 50g balls of 4-ply yarn main shade – white (MC)
3(4:4:5:5) x 50g balls of 4-ply yarn in contrast shade – red (A)
2(3:3:4:4) x 50g balls of 4-ply yarn in contrast shade – black (B)
1 x 50g ball of 4-ply yarn in contrast shade yellow (C)
Small amounts of contrast shades – wine (D), silver (E), blue (F) and grey (G)
1 pair each of 2.75mm and 3.25mm knitting needles
The quantities of yarn given are based on average requirements and are therefore approximate.

TENSION

28 stitches and 36 rows to 10cm square over st st on 3.25mm needles (or size needed to obtain given tension).

ABBREVIATIONS

alt = alternate; **beg** = beginning; **cont** = continue; **dec** = decrease; **foll** = following; **inc** = increase; **K** = knit; **P** = purl; **patt** = pattern; **rem** = remaining **rep** = repeat; **RS** = right side; **st(s)** = stitch(es); **st st** = stocking stitch; **tog** = together; **WS** = wrong side.

STRIPE PATTERN 1

1 row B, 2 rows C, 1 row B.

BACK

With 2.75mm needles and A, cast on 126(132:140:146:152) sts.
Work in K2, P2 rib for 26 rows.
Change to 3.25mm needles and MC, and starting with a K row, work in st st. Cont straight until work measures 39(42:46:50:54) cm from beg, ending with a P row.

Shape armholes

Inc 1 st at both ends of next and every foll 10th row, 6 times. [140(146:154:160:166) sts.]
Work 5(5:7:7:7) rows straight.

Shape shoulders

Cast off 7(7:6:7:7) sts at beg of next 12(12:14:14:14) rows, and 4(6:9:5:7) sts at beg of next 2 rows.
Leave rem 48(50:52:52:54) sts on a holder.

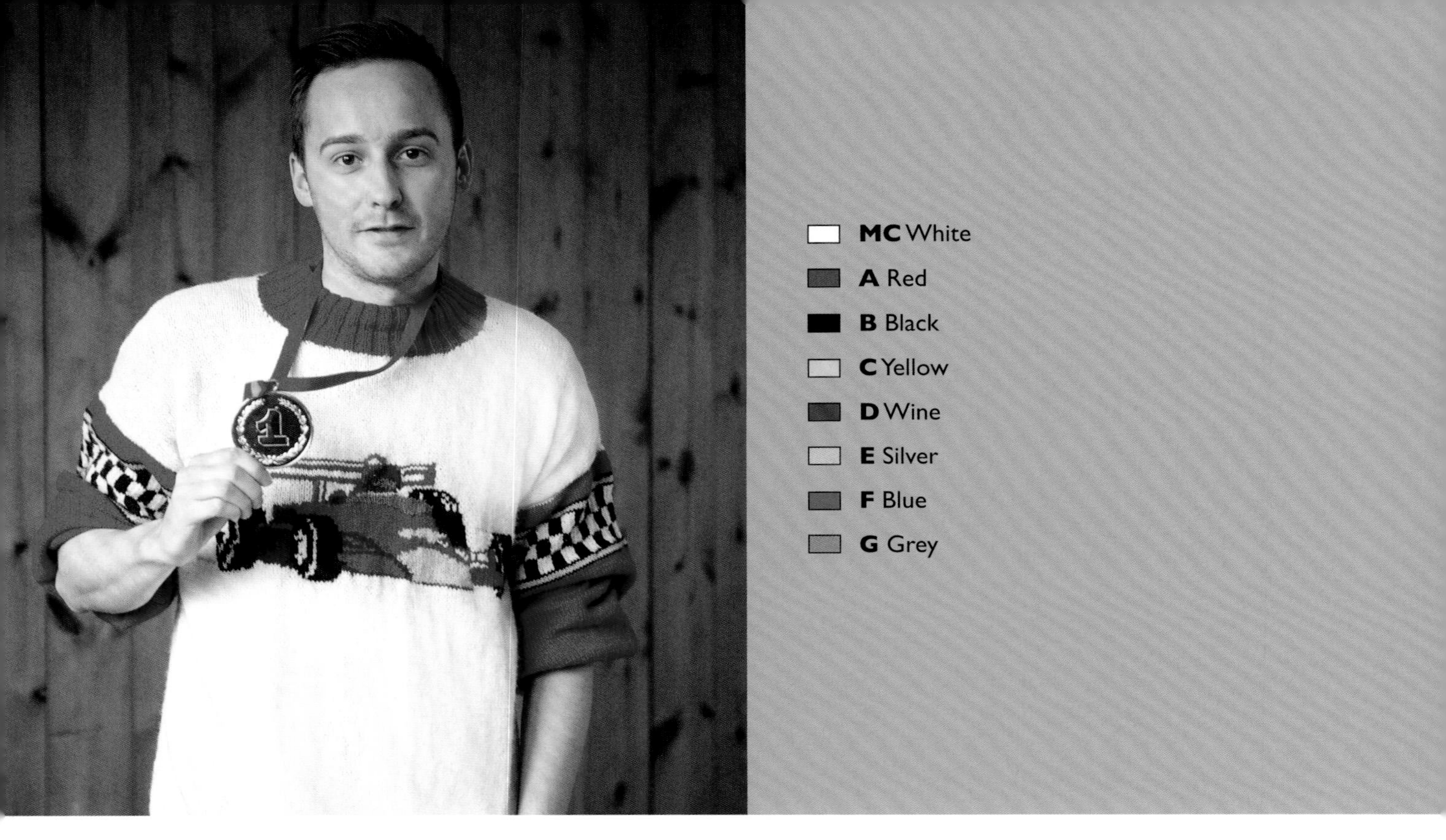

FRONT

Work as given for back until work measures 30(33:37:41:45)cm from beg, ending with a P row.

Next row: K19(22:26:29:32) sts, K 1st row of patt from chart, K to end of row.

Next row: P9(12:16:19:22) sts, P 2nd row of patt from chart, P to end of row.

Cont working rows of patt from chart as placed.

At the same time: When work measures same as back to armholes, shape armholes.

Shape armholes

Inc 1 st at both ends of next and every foll 10th row 6 times.

At the same time: When work measures 52(55:59:63:67)cm from beg, shape neck.

Shape neck

With RS of work facing, K55(57:62:65:67) sts, turn, leave rem sts on a spare needle. * Dec 1 st at neck edge on next 11(11:12:12:12) rows.

Work straight until length measures same as back to shoulder, ending at armhole edge.

Shape shoulder

Cast off 7(7:6:7:7) sts at beg of next and foll 5(5:6:6:6) alt rows.

Work 1 row.

Cast off 4(6:9:5:7) sts

With RS of work facing, slip next 26(28:28:28:30) sts onto a holder.

Rejoin yarn to next st and K to end of row.

Complete to match first side from * to end.

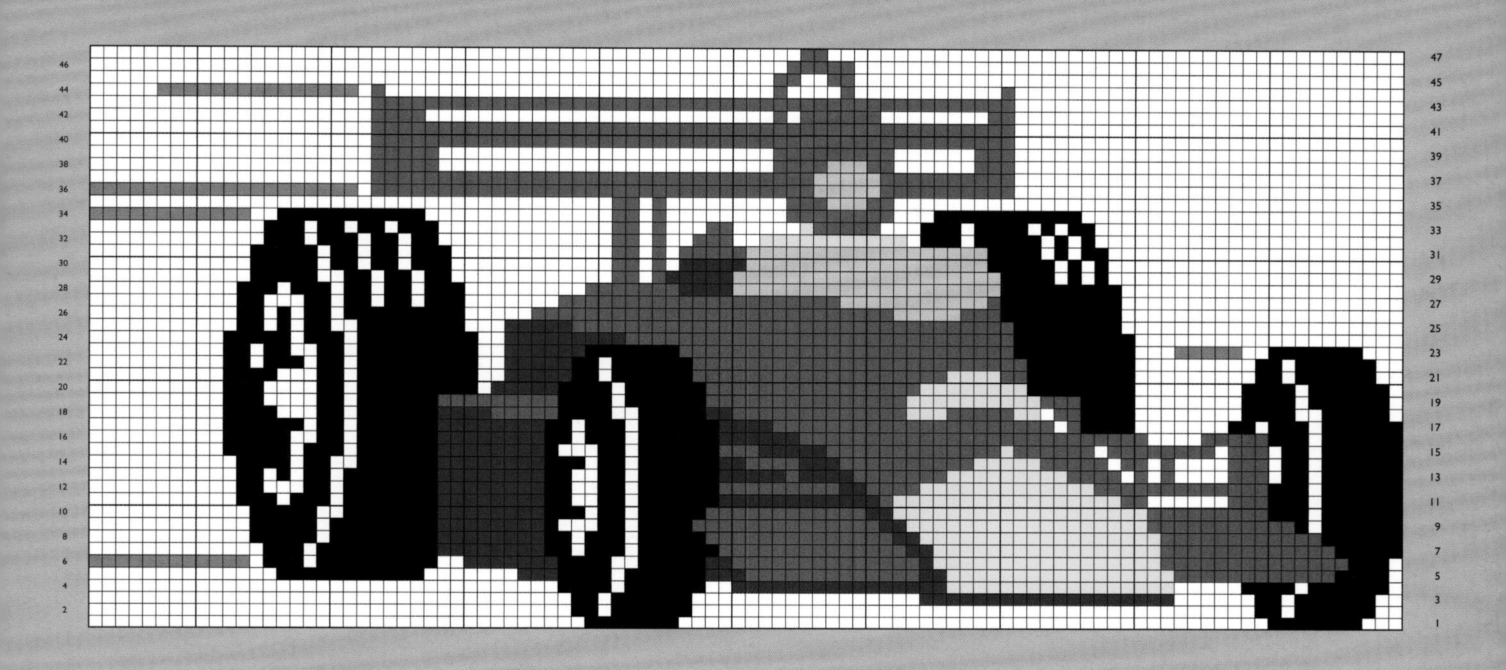

SLEEVES (both alike)

With 2.75mm needles and A, cast on 64(64:68:68:68) sts.

Work in K2, P2 rib for 26 rows. On the last row inc 48(48:52:52:52) sts evenly. [112(112:120:120:120) sts.]

Change to 3.25mm needles and, starting with a K row, work in st st. Cont straight until sleeve measures 29(32:32:32:34)cm from beg, ending with a P row.

Work rows of Stripe Pattern 1, then work chequers pattern as follows:

** **Row 1:** * K4 MC, K4 B, rep from * to end.

Row 2: * P4 B, P4 MC, rep from * to end.

Rep last 2 rows twice more.

Row 7: K4 B, K4 MC, rep from * to end.

Row 8: * P4 MC, P4 B, rep from * to end.

Rep last 2 rows twice more, then first 2 rows 3 times. (18 rows in all). **

Work rows of Stripe Pattern 1. Rejoin yarn A and work 8 rows. Break off A and work 3 rows MC.

Cast off.

NECKBAND

Sew up left shoulder seam.

With 2.75mm needles and A, pick up and knit 48(50:52:52:54) sts from back neck, 22(22:24:24:24) sts from left side neck, 26(28:28:28:30) sts from centre front and 22(22:24:24:24) sts from right side neck. [118(122:128:128:132) sts.].

Work in K2, P2 rib for 23 rows.

Cast off loosely in rib.

TO MAKE UP

Press work according to yarn instructions, omitting ribbing. Sew up right shoulder and neckband. Fold neckband in half and sew down on wrong side. Sew in sleeves. Sew up side and sleeve seams.

Full steam ahead

Vassos Alexander brightens up the daily commute for millions of listeners as part of the team on The Chris Evans Breakfast Show *on BBC Radio 2. Here he is brightening up our already sparkling steam train jumper – originally created by George Hostler for Gyles Brandreth to wear when he was hosting* The Railway Carriage Game *on BBC1 back in the early 1980s. This is a garment guaranteed to get any day started on the right track.*

MEASUREMENTS

To fit chest/bust: 87(92:97:102:107)cm
Length: 67(67:70:72:73)cm
Sleeve length: 48cm
Figures in brackets refer to the larger sizes.
Where only one figure is given this refers to all sizes.

MATERIALS

7(7:8:9:9) x 50g balls of 4-ply yarn in main shade – yellow (A)
3 x 50g balls of 4-ply yarn in contrast shade – white (B)
Small amounts of contrast shades – silver (C), black (D), grey (E), red (F), dark red (G), gold (H)
1 pair each of 2.75mm and 3.25mm knitting needles
The quantities of yarn given are based on average requirements and are therefore approximate.

TENSION

28 sts and 36 rows to 10cm square over st st on 3.25mm needles (or size needed to obtain given tension).

ABBREVIATIONS

alt = alternate; **beg** = beginning; **cont** = continue; **dec** = decrease; **foll** = following; **inc** = increase; **K** = knit; **k2tog** = knit 2 stitches together; **P** = purl; **p2tog** = purl 2 stitches together; **patt** = pattern; **psso** = pass slipped stitch over; **rem** = remaining **rep** = repeat; **RS** = right side; **s** = slip; **st(s)** = stitch(es); **st st** = stocking stitch; **tog** = together; **WS** = wrong side.

BACK

With 2.75mm needles and A, cast on 128(132:140:148:152) sts. Work in K2, P2 rib for 7cm.
Change to 3.25mm needles and starting with a K row, work in st st.
Cont straight until work measures 32(32:34:35:36)cm from beg, ending with a P row.
Join in contrast shade B and work scallop rows as follows:
Row 1: K0(0:2:2:0) sts, * K3, K2 in contrast B, K3, rep from * to last 0(0:2:2:0) sts, K2.
Row 2: P0(0:2:2:0) sts, * P1, P6 in contrast B, P1, rep from * to last 0(0:2:2:0) sts, P2.
Work 18 rows in B. Rejoin main shade A.
Row 21: K0(0:2:2:0) sts, * K1, K6 in contrast B, K1, rep from * to last 0(0:2:2:0) sts, K2.
Row 22: P0(0:2:2:0) sts, * P3, P2 in contrast B, P3, rep from * to last 0(0:2:2:0) sts, P2.
With main shade A, cont straight until work measures 44(44:47:48:49)cm from beg, ending with a P row.

Shape armholes

** Cast off 6 sts at beg of next 2 rows. Dec 1 st at both ends of the next 10 rows. Dec 1 st at both ends of the foll 2 alt rows. [92(96:104:112:116) sts.] **.
Work straight until armhole measures 11cm, ending with a P row.

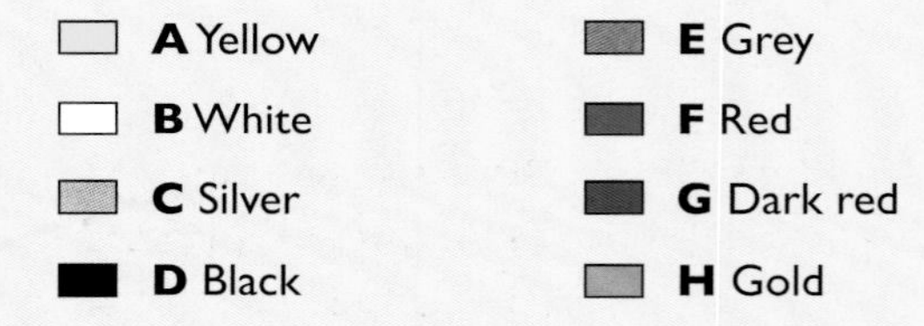

Join in contrast B and work scallop rows as follows:
Row 1: K2(0:0:0:2) sts, * K3, K2 in contrast B, K3, rep from * to last 2(0:0:0:2) sts, K2.
Row 2: P2(0:0:0:2) sts, * P1, P6 in contrast B, P1, rep from * to last 2(0:0:0:2) sts, P2.
Break off yarn A and complete in contrast B only.
Cont straight until armhole measures 23(23:23:24:24)cm.

Shape shoulders
Cast off 6(6:7:8:8) sts at beg of next 6 rows and 6(7:7:8:9) sts at beg of next 2 rows.
Leave rem 44(46:48:48:50) sts on a stitch holder.

FRONT
Work as given for back until work measures 31(31:33:34:35)cm from beg, ending with a P row.
Work next 93 rows of patt from chart.
At the same time: When work measures same as back to armholes, ending with a P row, shape armholes.

Shape armholes
Work as for back from ** to **. Work straight and when patt completed, cont in contrast B until armhole measures 18cm.

Shape neck

With RS of work facing, K34(35:38:42:43) sts, turn, leave rem sts on a spare needle.
*** Dec 1 st at neck edge on next 6 rows and foll 4 alt rows. [24(25:28:32:33) sts.]
Work straight until length measures same as back to shoulder, ending at armhole edge.

Shape shoulders

Cast off 6(6:7:8:8) sts at beg next and foll 2 alt rows.
Work 1 row. Cast off 6(7:7:8:9) sts.
With RS facing, slip next 24(26:28:28:30) sts onto a holder. Rejoin yarn to next st and K to end of row.
Complete to match first side from *** to end.

SLEEVES (both alike)

With 2.75mm needles and A, cast on 68 sts. Work in K2, P2 rib for 8cm.
Change to 3.25mm needles and, starting with a K row, work in st st.
Inc 1 st at both ends of next and every foll 6th row until there are 112 sts.
Work straight until sleeve measures 48cm or required length from beg, ending with a P row.

Shape top

Cast off 6 sts at beg of next 2 rows.
Dec 1 st at both ends of the next 8 rows.
Dec 1 st at both ends of every foll alt row until there are 54 sts.
Join in contrast B and work scallop rows as follows:
Row 1: s1, K1, psso, K1, * K3, K2 in contrast B, K3 *.
Rep from * to * 6 times.
K1, K2tog. [52 sts.]
Row 2: P2tog, * P1, P6 in contrast B, P1 *.
Rep from * to * 6 times.
P2tog. [50 sts.]

Break off A and complete in B. Dec 1 st at both ends of next 9 rows. Work 1 row.
Cast off 4 sts at beg of next 6 rows. Cast off rem 8 sts.

NECKBAND

Sew up left shoulder seam. With 2.75mm needles and contrast B and RS of work facing, pick up and knit 44(46:48:48:50) sts from back neck, 24 sts from left side neck, 24(26:28:28:30) sts from centre front, and 24 sts from right side neck. [116(120:124:124:128) sts.]
Work in K2, P2 rib for 5cm. Cast off loosely in rib.

TO MAKE UP

Press work according to yarn instructions, omitting ribbing. Sew up right shoulder and neckband. Fold neckband in half and sew down on WS. Set in sleeves, matching centre of sleeve top to shoulder seam, and scallop pattern to front and back. Sew up side and sleeve seams.

High flyer

The Wright brothers, Orville and Wilbur, are credited with flying the first aircraft to complete a controlled and sustained human flight on December 17th 1903. George Hostler is credited with fashioning this super stylish knit back on October 17th 1983. It's modelled here by the always high-flying James Hattsmith.

MEASUREMENTS

To fit chest/bust: 87(92:97:102:107)cm
Length: 61(65:67:69:71)cm
Sleeve length: 49(49:50:51:51)cm
Figures in brackets refer to the larger sizes.
Where only one figure is given this refers to all sizes.

MATERIALS

7(7:8:9:9) x 50g balls of 4-ply yarn in main shade – blue (A)
1 x 50g ball of 4-ply yarn in contrast shade – red (B)
3 x 50g balls of 4-ply yarn in contrast shade – white (C)
1 pair each of 2.75mm and 3.25mm knitting needles
The quantities of yarn given are based on average requirements and are therefore approximate.

TENSION

28 stitches and 36 rows to 10cm square over st st on 3.25mm needles (or size needed to obtain given tension).

ABBREVIATIONS

alt = alternate; **beg** = beginning; **cont** = continue; **dec** = decrease; **foll** = following; **inc** = increase; **K** = knit; **P** = purl; **patt** = pattern; **rem** = remaining **rep** = repeat; **RS** = right side; **st(s)** = stitch(es); **st st** = stocking stitch; **tog** = together; **WS** = wrong side.

BACK

With 2.75mm needles and main shade A, cast on 128(132:140:148:152) sts. Work in K2, P2 rib for 7cm.
Change to 3.25mm needles and, starting with a K row, work in st st.
Cont straight until work measures 20(24:26:27:29) cm from beg, ending with a K row.
** Join in contrast C and work 2 rows.
* Join in contrast B and work the 5 rows of Chart 2 across all sts. **
Rejoin in C and work 55 rows, rep. from * to ** once.
Work 2 rows C *****.
Rejoin in A and cont straight until work measures 42(46:48:49:51)cm from beg, ending with a P row.

Shape armholes

*** Inc 1 st at both ends of next and every foll 10th row, 6 times ***. [142(146:154:162:166) sts.]
Work 5(7:7:9:9) rows.

Shape shoulders

Cast off 6(6:6:7:7) sts at beg of next 14 rows and 5(6:9:6:7) sts at beg next 2 rows. Leave rem 48(50:52:52:54) sts on a holder.

FRONT

Work as for back until work measures 15(19:21:22:24)cm from beg, ending with a P row.

Next row: K9(11:15:19.21) sts, K 1st row of Chart 1, K to end.

Next row: P64(66:70:74:76) sts, P 2nd row of Chart 1, P to end.

Cont working rows of Chart 1 as placed.

When Chart 1 completed, work as back from * to **.

Work 2 rows C.

Next row: K18(20:24:28:30) sts, K 1st row of Chart 3, K to end.

Next row: P4(6:10:14:16) sts, P 2nd row of Chart 3, P to end.

Cont working rows of Chart 3 as placed.

When Chart 3 completed, work as back from * to **.

Work 2 rows C.

Next row: Join in A and K32(34:38:42:44) sts, K 1st row of Chart 4, K to end.

Next row: P64(66:70:74:76) sts, P 2nd row of Chart 4, P to end.

Cont working rows of Chart 4 as placed.

At the same time: When work measures same as back to armholes, ending with a P row, shape armholes.

Shape armholes

Work as back from *** to ***.

At the same time: When work measures 56(60:62:64:66)cm from beg, shape neck.

Shape neck

With RS of work facing, K57(59:52:66:67) sts, turn, leave rem sts on a spare needle.

**** Dec 1 st at neck edge on next 12 rows. Work straight until length measures same as back to shoulder, ending at armhole edge.

Shape shoulders

Cast off 6(6:6:7:7) sts at beg of next and foll 6 alt rows. Work 1 row.

Cast off 5(6:9:6:7) sts.

With RS of work facing, slip next 24(26:28:28:30) sts onto a holder. Rejoin yarn to next st and K to end of row.

Complete to match first side from **** to end.

SLEEVES (both alike)

With 2.75mm needles and main shade A, cast on 64(64:68:68:72) sts. Work in K2, P2 rib for 8cm. On the last row, inc 48(48:48:52:52) sts evenly. [112(112:116:120:120) sts.]

Change to 3.25mm needles and, starting with a K row, work in st st. Cont straight until work measures 26(26:28:29:29)cm from beg, ending with a K row. Work as back from ** to *****.

Rejoin in A and work 9 rows. Cast off.

NECKBAND

Sew up left shoulder seam. With RS of work facing and 2.75mm needles and main shade A, pick up and knit 48(50:52:52:54) sts from back neck, 24 sts from left side neck, 24(26:28:28:30) sts from centre front, and 24 sts from right side neck. [120(124:128:128:132) sts.]

Work in K2, P2 rib for 5cm.

Cast off loosely in rib.

TO MAKE UP

Press work according to yarn instructions, omitting ribbing. Sew up right shoulder and neckband. Fold neckband in half and sew down on WS. Sew in sleeves. Sew up side and sleeve seams.

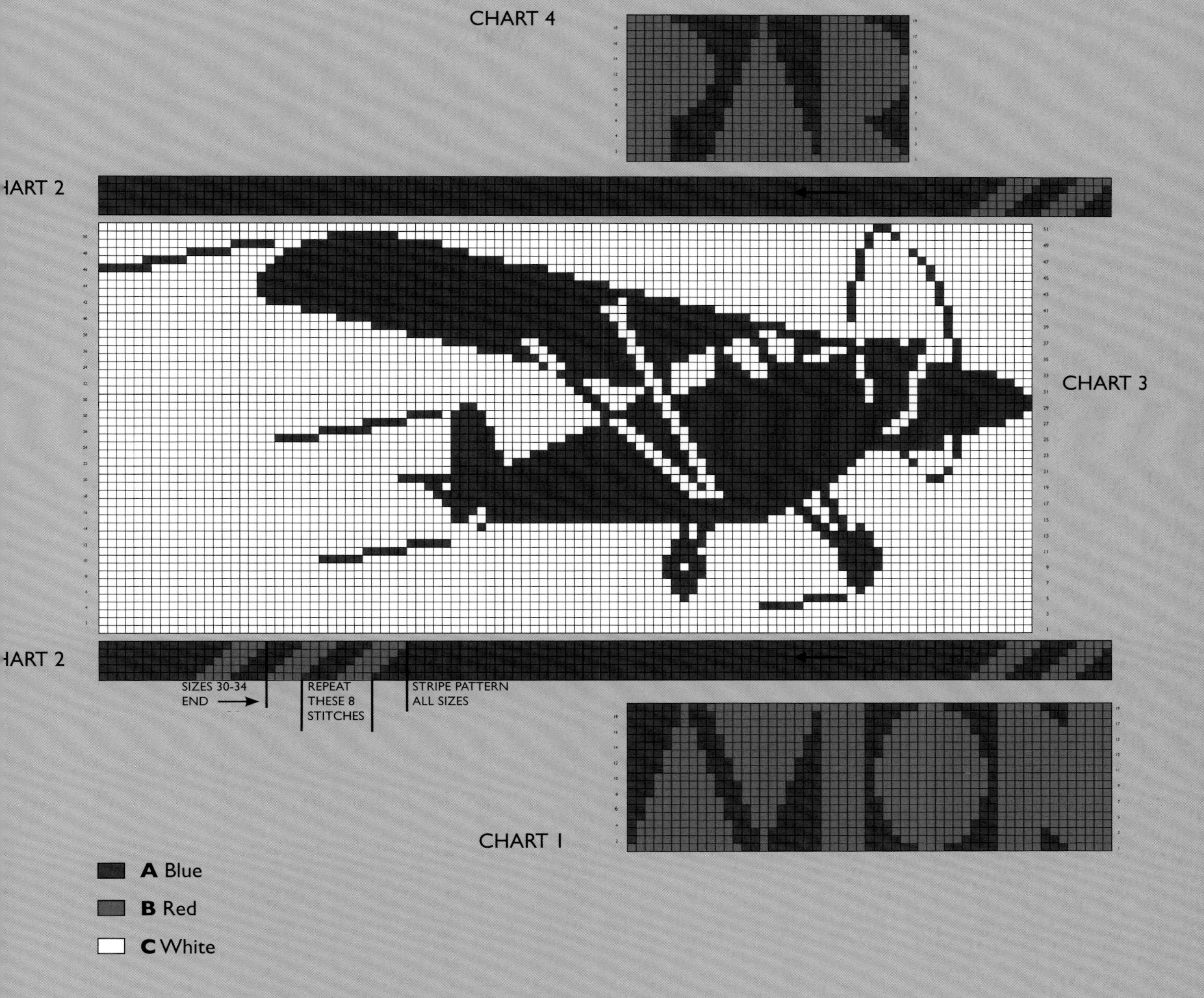

A Blue

B Red

C White

Bicycle made for one

Here is Martha Harlan looking wheel-y on-trend in this 'velocipedes' jumper (that's what they were called before the French coined the term bicycle in the 1860s). There may be over half a billion bicycles in China, but there's only one awesome bicycle jumper in Novelty Knits, *designed by the one and only Sarah Kim.*

MEASUREMENTS

To fit chest/bust: 81(86:91:97:102:107:112)cm
Length: 68(69:70:71:72:73:74)cm
Sleeve length: 50cm
Figures in brackets refer to the larger sizes.
Where only one figure is given this refers to all sizes.

MATERIALS

7(8:9:9:10:10:11) x 50g balls of 4-ply yarn in main shade – red (MC)
Small amounts of 4-ply yarn in contrast shades – black (A), charcoal (B) and cream (C)
1 pair each of 2.75mm and 3.25mm knitting needles
2 stitch holders
2 stitch markers
The quantities of yarn given are based on average requirements and are therefore approximate.

TENSION

28 stitches and 36 rows to 10cm square over st st on 3.25mm needles (or size needed to obtain given tension).

ABBREVIATIONS

alt = alternate; **beg** = beginning; **cont** = continue; **dec** = decrease; **foll** = following; **inc** = increase; **K** = knit; **K2tog** = knit 2 together; **P** = purl; **P2tog** = purl 2 together; **patt** = pattern; **pm** = place marker; **psso** = pass slipped stitch over; **rem** = remaining; **rep** = repeat; **RS** = right side; **s** = slip; **st(s)** = stitch(es); **st st** = stocking stitch; **tbl** = through back of loop; **tog** = together; **WS** = wrong side.

BACK

With 2.75mm needles and MC, use thumb method to cast on 123(129:135:147:153:159:165) sts.
Row 1 (RS): *K2, P1, rep from * to end.
Row 2: *K1, P2, rep from * to end.
Work 20 more rows in K2, P1 rib.
Change to 3.25mm needles and proceed as follows:
Row 1: K.
Row 2: P.
Working in st st, cont until back measures 38(39:40:41:42:43:44)cm, ending with a WS row.

Shape armholes

Row 1: K1, s1, K1, psso, K to last 3 sts, K2tog, K1. 121(127:133:145:151:157:163) sts.
Row 2: P1, P2tog, P to last 3 sts, P2tog tbl, P1. [119(125:131:143:149:155:161) sts.]
Rows 1 and 2 set dec for armholes.

Work 6 rows dec 1 st as before at each end of every row. [107(113:119:131:137:143:149) sts.]
** Cont in st st without shaping until armhole measures 24cm ending with WS row.

Shape shoulders

Cast off 6(7:7:8:9:9:10) sts at beg next 8 rows, then cast off 5(4:6:7:6:8:7) sts at beg next 2 rows. [49(49:51:53:53:55:55) sts.]
Leave rem 49(49:51:53:53:55:55) sts on a stitch holder.

PLACEMENT OF CHART

Follow patt for front as below until work measures 24(25:26:27:28:29:30)cm ending with a WS row.
Next row: K17(20:23:29:32:35:38) sts in MC, pm, K across 90 sts of 1st row of chart, pm, K across rem of row in MC. This row shows placement of chart. Complete 80 rows of chart.
At the same time: Cont working front patt shapings.

FRONT

Work as given for Back to **. Cont in st st without shaping until armhole measures 16cm, ending with WS row.

Shape neck

Next row: K39(42:44:49:52:54:57), K2tog, turn, leave rem 66(69:73:80:83:87:90) sts on a stitch holder. Working on these 40(43:45:50:53:55:58) sts only, proceed as follows:
Next row: P2tog, P to end. [39(42:44:49:52:54:57) sts.]
Work 10 rows dec 1 st as before at neck edge in every row. [29(32:34:39:42:44:47) sts.]
Cont straight until front measures the same as back to beg of shoulder shaping, ending with WS row.
Cast off 6(6:7:8:8:9:9) sts at beg of next and foll 3 alt rows. [5(8:6:7:10:8:11) sts.]
Work 1 row. Cast off rem 5(8:6:7:10:8:11) sts. With RS facing, working on rem 66(69:73:80:83:87:90) sts, slip 25(25:27:28:30:31:31) sts onto a stitch holder, rejoin yarn to rem 41(44:46:51:54:56:59), K2tog, K to end of row. [40(43:45:50:53:55:58) sts.]
Next row: P to last 2 sts, P2tog tbl. [39(42:44:49:52:54:57) sts.]
Work 10 rows dec 1 st as before at neck edge in every row. [29(32:34:39:42:44:47) sts.]
Cont straight until front measures the same as back to beg of shoulder shaping, ending with RS row.
Cast off 6(6:7:8:8:9:9) sts at beg of next and foll 3 alt rows. [5(8:6:7:10:8:11) sts.]
Work 1 row. Cast off rem 5(8:6:7:10:8:11) sts.

SLEEVES (both alike)

With 2.75mm needles and MC, use thumb method to cast on 69 sts, work 22 rows in K2, P1 rib.
Change to 3.25mm needles and working in st st, inc 1 st at each end of 6th and every foll 4th row to 133 sts. Cont without shaping until sleeve measures 48cm, or length required, ending with a WS row.

Shape armholes

Row 1: K1, s1, K1, psso, K to last 3 sts, K2tog, K1. [131 sts.]
Row 2: P1, P2tog, P to last 2 sts, P2tog tbl, P1. [129 sts.]
Rows 1 and 2 set armhole shapings. Work 6 rows, dec 1 st as before at each end every row. [117 sts.]
Cast off.

NECKBAND

Join left shoulder seam.

With RS facing, using MC and 2.75mm needles, work across 49(49:51:53:53:55:55) sts left on stitch holder at back of neck, pick up and knit 23(25:24:24:24:25:25) sts evenly along left side of neck, work across 25(25:27:29:29:31:31) sts left on stitch holder at front of neck, pick up and knit 23(24:24:23:23:24:24) sts evenly along right side of neck. [120(123:126:129:129:135:135) sts.]

Starting with 2nd row of K2, P1 rib, work 12 rows.

Cast off in rib.

TO MAKE UP

With contrast shade A, use backstitch to embroider the spoke details onto the wheels of the bicycle as shown in the photograph on page 89. Join right shoulder and neckband seams. Sew in sleeves. Join side and sleeve seams. Weave in all ends. Pin out garment to the measurements given. Cover with damp cloths and leave until dry. See ball band for washing and further care instructions.

MC Red

A Black

B Charcoal

C Cream

Key to success

This piano keys jumper always hits the right note and it is perfectly in tune with our model, Kosha Engler. Miss Engler is a multi-talented actress and singer who, when she's not tickling our fancy, is a dab hand at tickling the ivories.

MEASUREMENTS

To fit chest/bust: 87(92:97:102:107)cm
Length: 61(65:67:69:71)cm
Sleeve length: 49(49:50:50:51)cm
Figures in brackets refer to the larger sizes.
Where only one figure is given this refers to all sizes.

MATERIALS

7(7:8:9:9) x 50g balls of 4-ply yarn in main shade – red (A)
3 x 50g balls of 4-ply yarn in each of contrast shades – black (B) and white (C)
1 pair each of 2.75mm and 3.25mm knitting needles
The quantities of yarn given are based on average requirements and are therefore approximate.

TENSION

28 sts and 36 rows to 10cm square over st st on 3.25mm needles (or size needed to obtain given tension).

ABBREVIATIONS

alt = alternate; **beg** = beginning; **cont** = continue; **dec** = decrease; **foll** = following; **inc** = increas(e)ing; **K** = knit; **P** = purl; **patt** = pattern; **rem** = remaining **rep** = repeat; **RS** = right side; **st(s)** = stitch(es); **st st** = stocking stitch; **tog** = together; **WS** = wrong side.

BACK

With 2.75mm needles and A, cast on 129(135:141:147:153) sts. Work in K2, P2 rib for 7cm.
Change to 3.25mm needles and starting with a K row, work in st st. Cont straight until work measures 22(26:28:29:31)cm from beg, ending with a P row.
Join in contrast B and C and work rows of patt from chart.
Rejoin in A and cont straight until work measures 60(64:66:68:70)cm from beg, ending with a P row.

Shape armholes

* Inc 1 st at both ends of next and every foll 10th row, 6 times. [142(146:154:162:166) sts.]
Work 5(7:7:9:9) rows.

Shape shoulders

Cast off 6(6:6:7:7) sts at beg of next 14 rows, and 5(6:9:5:7) sts at beg of next 2 rows.
Leave rem 49(50:53:53:55) sts on a holder.

FRONT

Work as given for back to *.
At the same time: When work measures 56(60:62:64:66)cm from beg, shape neck.

Shape neck

With RS of work facing, K57(59:62:66:67) sts, turn, leave rem sts on a spare needle. ** Dec 1 st at neck edge

on next 12 rows. Work straight until length measures same as back to shoulder, ending at armhole edge.

Shape shoulders

Cast off 6(6:6:7:7) sts at beg of next and foll 6 alt rows. Work 1 row. Cast off 5(6:9:5:7) sts.
With RS of work facing, slip the next 25(26:29:29:31) sts onto a stitch holder.
Rejoin yarn to next st and K to end of row.
Complete to match first side from ** to end.

SLEEVES (both alike)

With 2.75mm needles and A, cast on 68(68:70:70:72) sts. Work in K2, P1 rib for 5cm.
Change to 3.25mm needles and, starting with a K row, work in st st, inc at each end of 5th and every foll 4th row until work measures 30(30:31:31:32)cm from beg, ending with a P row.
Join in contrasts B and C and work rows of patt as foll:
Row 1: K0(0:2:2:4), K the rep patt on chart (twice), K0(0:2:2:4)
Row 2: P0(0:2:2:4), P the rep patt on chart (twice), P0(0:2:2:4)
At the same time: Cont inc until there are 126(126:130:130:136) sts.
When patt completed, rejoin in main shade A and work 9 rows.
Cast off.

NECKBAND

Sew up left shoulder seam.
With 2.75mm needles and main shade A, and RS of work facing, pick up and knit 49(50:53:53:55) sts from back neck, 24 sts from left side neck, 25(26:29:29:31) sts from centre front and 25(23:23:23:25) sts from right side neck [123(123:129:129:135) sts.]
Work in K2, P1 rib for 5cm. Cast off loosely in rib.

TO MAKE UP

Press work according to yarn instructions, omitting ribbing. Sew up right shoulder and neckband. Fold neckband in half and sew down on wrong side.
Mark 22(22:23:23:24)cm down from shoulder seams. Sew in sleeves between marks. Sew up side and sleeve seams.

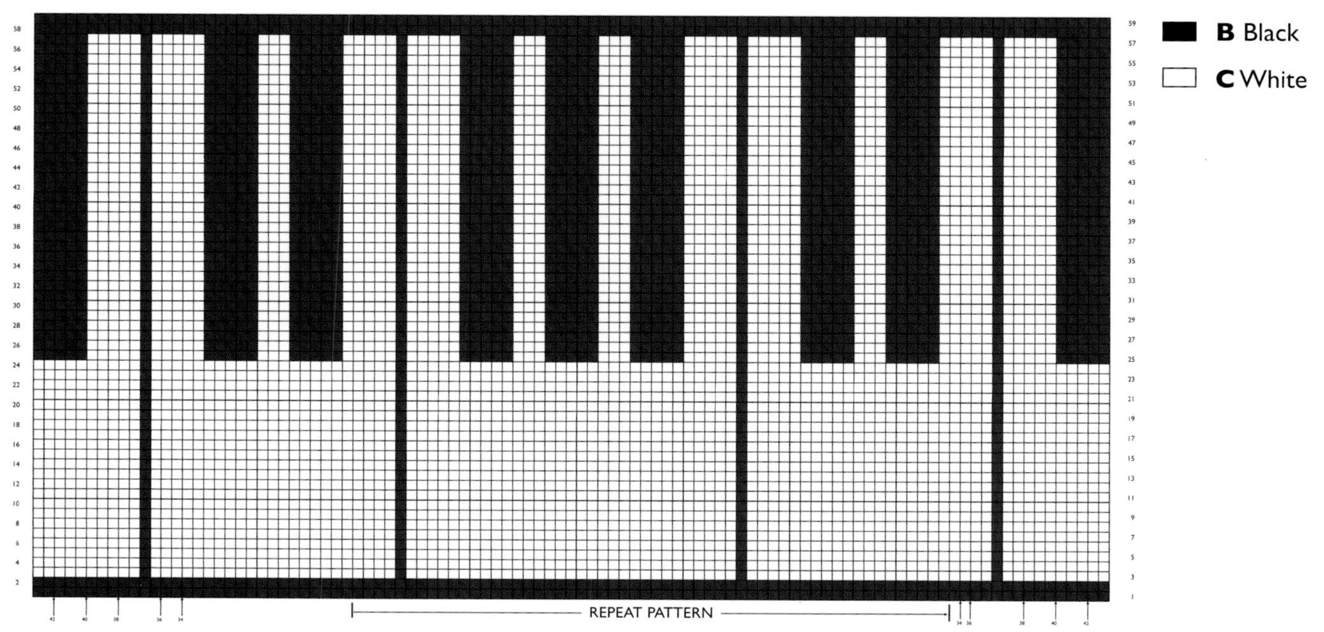

Ravishing robot

Here we have the multi-talented Justine Roberts in our red hot robot jumper. Justine has harnessed the power of modern technology with her phenomenally successful website Mumsnet, which gives parents a chance to swap tips, advice and opinions. It launched in 2000 with the slogan 'by parents for parents' and by 2013 she, and her co-founder Carrie Longton, were named by Woman's Hour *as the seventh most influential women in the UK. Getting her to model for us, and Women for Women International, seemed a perfect fit… just like this cute cropped jumper.*

MEASUREMENTS

To fit chest/bust: 87(92:97:102:107)cm
Length: 56(58:61:64:66)cm
Sleeve length: 47(48:48:49:49)cm
Figures in brackets refer to the larger sizes.
Where only one figure is given this refers to all sizes.

MATERIALS

8(9:10:11:12) x 50g balls of 4-ply yarn in main shade – red (A)
1 x 50g balls of 4-ply yarn in contrast shade – grey (B)
Small amounts of 4-ply yarn in each of contrast shades – black (C), white (D), orange (E), yellow (F), green (G), blue (H) and violet (I)
1 pair each of 2.75mm and 3.25mm knitting needles
The quantities of yarn given are based on average requirements and are therefore approximate.

TENSION

28 stitches and 36 rows to 10cm square over st st on 3.25mm needles (or size needed to obtain given tension).

ABBREVIATIONS

alt = alternate; **beg** = beginning; **cont** = continue; **dec** = decrease; **foll** = following; **inc** = increas(e)ing; **K** = knit; **P** = purl; **patt** = pattern; **rem** = remaining; **rep** = repeat; **RS** = right side; **st(s)** = stitch(es); **st st** = stocking stitch; **tbl** = through back of loop; **tog** = together; **WS** = wrong side.

BACK

With 2.75mm needles and A, cast on 131(137:143:149:155) sts and work in K2, P1 rib for 4cm.
Change to 3.25mm needles and work in st st, increasing 1 st in the first row.
[132(138:144:150:156) sts.]
Cont straight until work measures 35(36:38:40:42) cm from beg, ending with a P row.

Shape armholes

Cast off 7(9:9:11:11) sts at beg of the next two rows. [118(120:126:128:134) sts.]
Cont straight until armhole measures 21(22:23:24:24)cm, ending with a P row.

Shape shoulders

Starting with the RS, cast off 12(12:15:15:18) sts at beg of the next row, K24, dec 1 st.
Put next 42(44:44:46:48) sts onto a stitch holder (centre back neck sts) and rem sts onto another stitch holder (left side shoulder sts).
Next row: Dec 1, K11, cast off 12 sts.
Next row: K12.
Next row: Cast off 12 sts.
Reverse shoulder shapings for the left side.

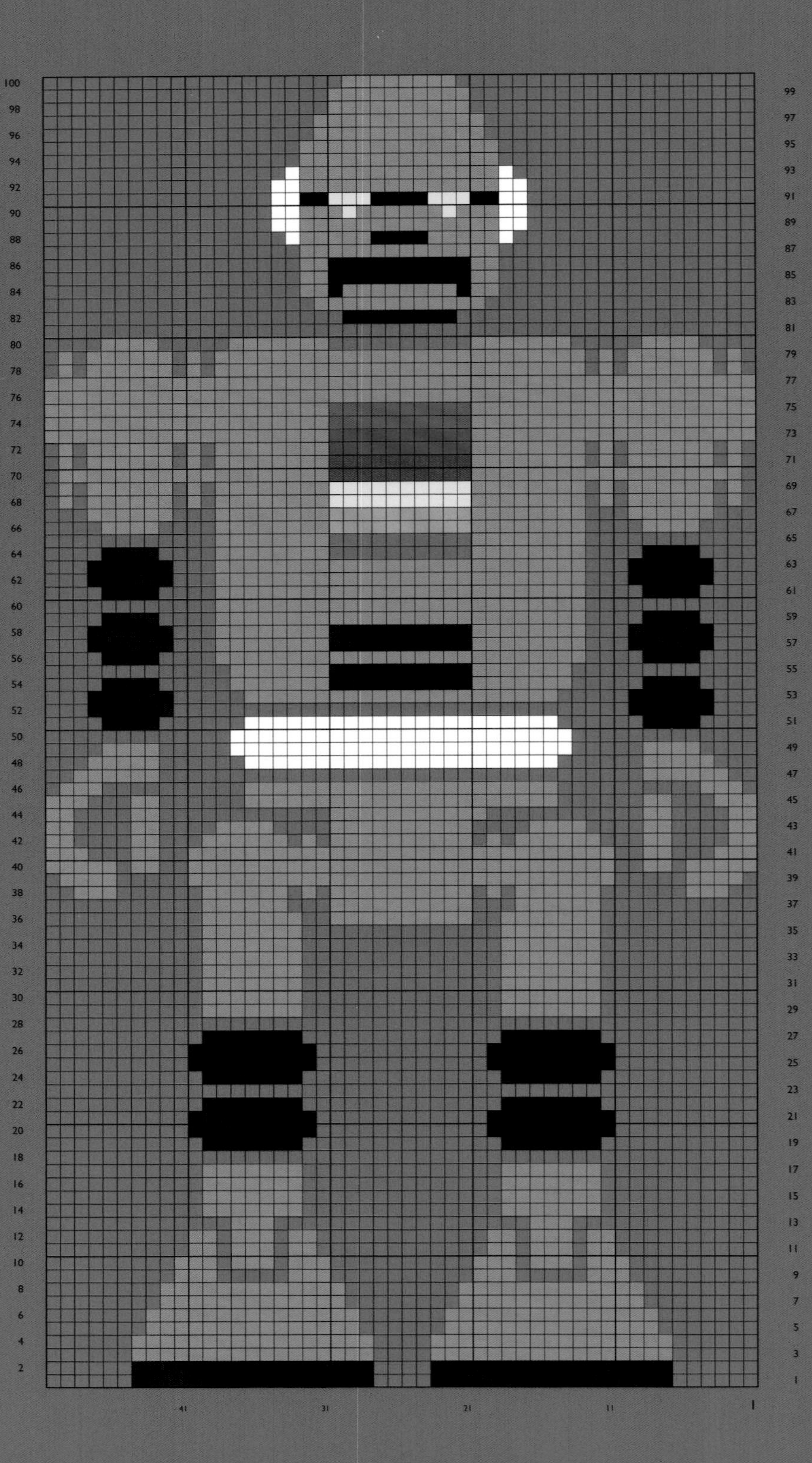

- **A** Red
- **B** Grey
- **C** Black
- **D** White
- **E** Orange
- **F** Yellow
- **G** Green
- **H** Blue
- **I** Violet

FRONT

Work as given for back until work measures 12(13:15:16:17)cm from beg, ending with a P row.

Next row: K41(44:47:50:53) sts, K 1st row of patt from chart, K to end of row.

Next row: P41(44:47:50:53) sts, P 2nd row of patt from chart, P to end of row.

Cont working rows of patt from chart as placed.

At the same time: When work measures same as back to armholes, shape armholes as for back and when work measures 50(52:55:58:60)cm from beg, shape neck.

Shape neck

With RS of work facing, K48(48:48:50:51) sts. Put next 22(24:24:26:26) sts onto a stitch holder (centre front neck sts) and rem 48(48:48:50:51) sts onto a stitch holder or spare needle

Next row: ** P2, dec 1 st, P to end.

Next 8 rows: Dec 1 st at the neck edge on every row.

Next row: K.

Next row: Dec 1 st at the neck edge.

Rep the last 2 rows twice more.

Knit 6 rows.

Shape shoulder

Cast off 12(12:15:15:18) sts, K24, dec 1 st.

Next row: Dec 1 st, K11, cast off 12 sts.

Next row: K12.

Next row: Cast off 12 sts.

Rejoin yarn to first st of the 48(48:48:50:51) sts for the left side and complete to match the first side reversing the sts from ** to end.

SLEEVES (both alike)

With 2.75mm needles and A, cast on 62(62:69:69:69) sts. Work in K2, P1 rib for 4cm.

Change to 3.25mm needles.

Inc row: K inc 9(9:10:10:10) sts evenly across row.

[71(71:79:79:79) sts.]

Cont in st st for 5 rows and inc 1 st at each end of the next row. Cont inc in this way every 6th row until you have 113(119:125:131:131) sts.

Cont straight until work measures 47(48:48:49:49)cm.

Cast off.

NECKBAND

Sew up left shoulder seam. With RS of work facing and 2.75mm needles and A, pick up and knit 23 sts from right side neck, 22(24:24:26:26) sts from stitch holder (front neck) 23 sts from left side neck, 2 sts from back left neck, 42(44:44:46:48) sts from stitch holder (back neck), 2 sts from back right neck. [114(118:118:122:124) sts.]

Work in K2, P1 rib for 5cm.

Cast off loosely in rib.

TO MAKE UP

Press work according to band instructions, omitting ribbing. Sew up right shoulder and neckband. Fold neckband in half and sew down on wrong side. Sew in sleeves. Sew up side and sleeve seams.

Watch the birdie

This golfing jumper was originally modelled for us by Jane Asher. Getting into the swing of things this time round is Kosha Engler, who assures us compliments are par for the course when she sports this stylish knit down at the club.

MEASUREMENTS

To fit chest/bust: 87(92:97:102:107)cm
Length: 62(66:69:70:71)cm
Sleeve length: 48cm
Figures in brackets refer to the larger sizes.
Where only one figure is given this refers to all sizes.

MATERIALS

9(9:10:11:11) x 50g balls of 4-ply yarn in main shade – blue (A)
Small amounts of contrast shades for golfer – just remember to use lighter and darker shades of the same colour for his jumper and trousers to give him form.
1 pair each of 2.75mm and 3.25mm knitting needles
The quantities of yarn given are based on average requirements and are therefore approximate.

TENSION

28 stitches and 36 rows to 10cm square over st st on 3.25mm needles (or size needed to obtain given tension).

ABBREVIATIONS

alt = alternate; **beg** = beginning; **cont** = continue; **dec** = decrease; **foll** = following; **inc** = increase; **K** = knit; **P** = purl; **patt** = pattern; **rem** = remaining **rep** = repeat; **RS** = right side; **st(s)** = stitch(es); **st st** = stocking stitch; **tog** = together; **WS** = wrong side.

BACK

With 2.75mm needles and main shade A, cast on 129(132:141:147:153) sts. Work in K2, P1 rib for 6cm.
Change to 3.25mm needles and, starting with a K row, work in st st. Cont straight until work measures 38(42:44:46:47) cm from beg, ending with a P row.

Shape armholes

* Dec 1 st at both ends on next 8 rows. *
[113(116:125:131:137) sts.]
Work straight until armhole measures 24cm.

Shape shoulders

Cast off 7(7:7:8:8) sts at beg of next 8 rows, and 4(5:8:7:9) sts at beg next 2 rows. Leave rem 49(50:53:53:55) sts on holder.

FRONT

Work as given for back until work measures 11(15:18:19:20)cm from beg, ending with a P row.
Next row: K47(49:53:56:59) sts, K 1st row of patt from chart, K to end.
Next row: P22(23:28:31:34) sts, P 2nd row of patt from chart, P to end.
Cont working rows of patt from the chart as placed.
At the same time: When work measures same as back to armholes, ending with a P row, shape armholes.

The gorgeous Jane Asher sporting our equally gorgeous golfer knit in 1986.

Shape armholes

Work as given for back from * to *, keeping patt over sts as set. Work straight until armhole measures 16cm.

Shape neck

With RS of work facing, K44(45:48:57:53) sts, turn, leave rem sts on a spare needle.
** Dec 1 st at neck edge on the next 12 rows.
Work straight until length measures same as back to shoulder, ending at armhole edge.

Shape shoulders

Cast off 7(7:7:8:8) sts at beg of next and foll 3 alt rows. Work 1 row.
Cast off 4(5:8:7:9) sts.
With RS of work facing, slip next 25(26:29:29:31) sts onto a holder. Rejoin yarn to next st and K to end of row.
Complete to match first side from ** to end.

SLEEVES (both alike)

With 2.75mm needles and A, cast on 69 sts. Work in K2, P1 rib for 7cm.
Change to 3.25mm needles and, starting with a K row, work in st st, inc 1 st at both ends of the 6th and every foll 4th row until there are 133 sts.
Work straight until sleeve measures 48cm from beg, ending with a P row.

Shape armholes

Dec 1 st at both ends on the next 8 rows. [117 sts.]
Cast off.

NECKBAND

Sew up left shoulder seam. With 2.75mm needles and A, and RS of work facing, pick up and knit 49(50:53:53:55) sts from back neck, 24 sts from left side neck, 25(26:29:29:31) sts from centre front and 25(23:23:23:25) sts from right side neck. [123(123:129:129:135) sts.]
Work in K2, P1 rib for 5cm. Cast off loosely in rib.

TO MAKE UP

Press work according to yarn instructions, omitting ribbing. Sew up right shoulder and neckband.
Fold neckband in half and sew down on wrong side.
Sew in sleeves. Sew up side and sleeve seams.

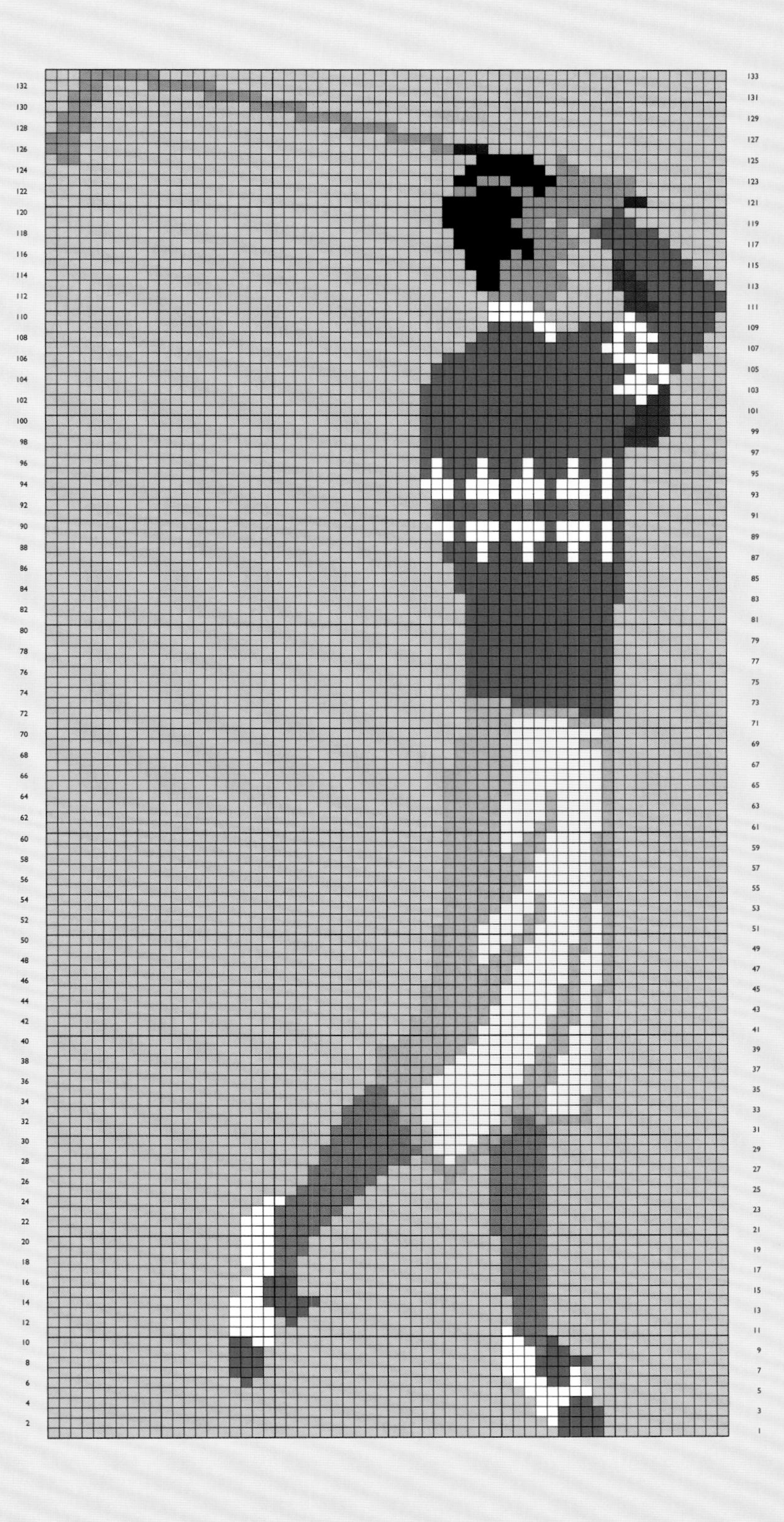

A Blue
B Red
C White
D Grey
E Fawn
F Cream
G Dark red
H Mushroom
I Black
J Dark brown
K Silver

Anchors away

We're all at sea for this nautical knit. Another updated Hostler classic, here is it being modelled on the port side by Hugh Bonneville, and on the starboard by Saethryd Brandreth.

MEASUREMENTS

To fit chest/bust: 87(92:97:102:107)cm
Length: 61(65:67:69:71)cm
Sleeve length: 49(49:50:51:51)cm
Figures in brackets refer to the larger sizes. Where only one figure is given this refers to all sizes.

MATERIALS

9(9:10:11:11) x 50g balls of 4-ply yarn in main shade – navy (A)
1 x 50g ball of 4-ply yarn in contrast shade – white (B)
Small amount of contrast shade – red (C)
1 pair each of 2.75mm and 3.25mm knitting needles
The quantities of yarn given are based on average requirements and are therefore approximate.

TENSION

28 stitches and 36 rows to 10cm square over st st on 3.25mm needles (or size needed to obtain given tension).

ABBREVIATIONS

alt = alternate; **beg** = beginning; **cont** = continue; **dec** = decrease; **foll** = following; **inc** = increase; **K** = knit; **P** = purl; **patt** = pattern; **rem** = remaining **rep** = repeat; **RS** = right side; **st(s)** = stitch(es); **st st** = stocking stitch; **tog** = together; **WS** = wrong side.

BACK

With 2.75mm needles and A, cast on 128(132:140:148:152) sts. Work in K2, P2 rib for 7cm.
Change to 3.25mm needles and, starting with a K row, work in st st.
Cont straight until work measures 42(46:48:49:51)cm from beg, ending with a P row.

Shape armholes

* Inc 1 st at both ends of the next and every foll 10th row 6 times *. [142(146:154:162:166) sts.]
Work 5(7:7:9:9) rows straight.

Shape shoulders

Cast off 6(6:6:7:7) sts at beg of next 14 rows and 5(6:9:6:7) sts at beg next 2 rows. Leave rem 48(50:52:52:54) sts on a stitch holder.

FRONT

Work as given for back until work measures 14(18:20:22:24)cm from beg, ending with a P row.
Next row: K34(36:40:44:46) sts, K 1st row of patt from chart, K to end of row.
Next row: P35(37:41:45:47) sts, P 2nd row of patt from chart, P to end of row.
Cont working rows of patt as placed.
At the same time: When work measures same as back to armholes, ending with a P row, shape armholes.

Shape armholes

Work as given for back from * to *.
At the same time: When work measures 56(60:62:64:66)cm from beg, shape neck.

Shape neck

With RS of work facing, K57(59:62:66:67) sts, turn, leave rem sts on a spare needle.
** Dec 1 st at neck edge on the next 12 rows.
Work straight until length measures same as back to shoulder, ending at armhole edge.

A Navy

B White

C Red

Shape shoulders

Cast off 6(6:6:7:7) sts at beg of next and foll 6 alt rows. Work 1 row.
Cast off 5(6:9:6:7) sts.
With RS of work facing, slip next 24(26:28:28:30) sts onto a holder. Rejoin yarn to next st and K to end of row.
Complete to match first side from ** to end.

SLEEVES (both alike)

With 2.75mm needles and A, cast on 64(64:68:68:72) sts. Work in K2, P2 rib for 8cm.
On the last row, inc 48(48:48:52:52) sts evenly.
[112(112:116:120:124) sts.]
Change to 3.25mm needles and, starting with a K row, work in st st.
Cont straight until work measures 49(49:50:51:51) cm from beg.
Cast off.

NECKBAND

Sew up left shoulder seam. With RS of work facing and 2.75mm needles, pick up and knit 48(50:52:52:54) sts from back neck, 24 sts from left side neck, 24(26:28:28:30) sts from centre front, and 24 sts from right side neck.
[120(124:128:128:132) sts.]
Work in K2, P2 rib for 5cm.
Cast off loosely in rib.

TO MAKE UP

Press work according to yarn instructions, omitting ribbing. Sew up right shoulder and neckband. Fold neckband in half and sew down on wrong side. Sew in sleeves. Sew up side and sleeve seams.

Show jumper

Have you heard the one about the horse with a negative attitude? It always said 'neigh!' Luckily for us Emma McQuiston said 'yes' to modelling this stylish sweater, first worn for us by Joanna Lumley. The book-ish background is particularly apt as Emma, in her role as Viscountess Weymouth, lives at Longleat, a magnificent stately home in Wiltshire, England, which not only houses Europe's first safari park but also one of the continent's largest private book collections, with seven libraries and over 40,000 books.

MEASUREMENTS

To fit chest/bust: 87(92:97:102:107)cm
Length: 62(66:69:70:71)cm
Sleeve length: 48cm
Figures in brackets refer to the larger sizes.
Where only one figure is given this refers to all sizes.

MATERIALS

4 x 50g balls of 4-ply yarn in main shade – red (A)
3 x 50g balls of 4-ply yarn in contrast shade – dark green (B)
4 x 50g balls of 4-ply yarn in contrast shade – cream (C)
Small amounts of brown, black, tan, beige and dark red
1 pair each of 2.75mm and 3.25mm knitting needles
The quantities of yarn given are based on average requirements and are therefore approximate.

TENSION

28 stitches and 36 rows to 10cm square over st st on 3.25mm needles (or size needed to obtain given tension).

ABBREVIATIONS

alt = alternate; **beg** = beginning; **cont** = continue; **dec** = decrease; **foll** = following; **inc** = increas(e)ing; **K** = knit; **P** = purl; **patt** = pattern; **rem** = remaining **rep** = repeat; **RS** = right side; **st(s)** = stitch(es); **st st** = stocking stitch; **tog** = together; **WS** = wrong side.

BACK

With 2.75mm needles and main shade A, cast on 128(132:140:148:152) sts. Work in K2, P2 rib for 7cm.
Change to 3.25mm needles and, starting with a K row, work in st st. Cont straight until work measures 14(18:20:21:23)cm from beg.
Break off A. Join in contrast B and cont straight for further 14cm, ending with a P row *.
Break off B. Join in contrast C and cont straight until work measures 38(42:44:46:47)cm from beg, ending with a P row.

Shape armholes

** Dec 1 st at both ends on next 8 rows. [112(116:124:132:136)sts.] **
Work straight until armhole measures 24cm.

NORMAN DAVIES
OUR KIND OF TRAITOR
SUGGS
MATISSE

Shape shoulders

Cast off 7(7:7:8:8) sts at beg of next 8 rows, and 4(5:8:8:9) sts at beg of next 2 rows.
Leave rem 48(50:52:52:54) sts on a stitch holder.

FRONT

Work as given for back to *.
Break off B. Join in C and work patt as follows:
Next row: K27(29:33:37:39) sts, K 1st row of patt from chart, K to end of row.
Next row: P13(15:19:23:25) sts, P 2nd row of patt from chart, P to end of row.
Cont working rows of patt from the chart as placed.
At the same time: When work measures same as back to armholes, ending with a P row, shape armholes.

Shape armholes

Work as given for back from ** to **. Work straight until armhole measures 16cm. Shape neck.

Shape neck

With RS of work facing, K44(45:48:52:54) sts, turn, leave rem sts on a spare needle.
*** Dec 1 st at neck edge on the next 12 rows.
Work straight until length measures same as back to shoulder, ending at armhole edge.

Shape shoulders

Cast off 7(7:7:8:8) sts at beg of next and foll 3 alt rows. Work 1 row.
Cast off 4(5:8:8:9) sts.
With RS of work facing, slip next 24(26:28:28:30) sts onto a holder. Rejoin yarn to next st and K to end of row.
Complete to match first side from *** to end.

SLEEVES (both alike)

With 2.75mm needles and main shade A, cast on 68 sts. Work in K2, P2 rib for 7cm.
Change to 3.25mm needles and, starting with a K row, work in st st, inc 1 st at both ends of the 6th and every foll 4th row.
When work measures 24cm from beg, break off A.
Join in contrast B and cont until work measures 38cm from beg, ending with a P row.
Break off B. Join in contrast C and cont inc until there are 132 sts.
Work straight until sleeve measures 48cm from beg, ending with a P row.

Shape armholes

Dec 1 st at both ends on next 8 rows. [116 sts.]
Cast off.

NECKBAND

Sew up left shoulder seam. With 2.75mm needles and RS of work facing, pick up and knit 48(50:52:52:54) sts from back neck, 24 sts from left side neck, 24(26:28:28:30) sts from centre front, and 24 sts from right side neck. [120(124:128:128:132) sts.].
Work in K2, P2 rib for 5cm. Cast off loosely in rib.

TO MAKE UP

Press work according to yarn instructions, omitting ribbing. Sew up right shoulder and neckband.
Fold neckband in half and sew down on WS.
Sew in sleeves. Sew up side and sleeve seams.

A Red

C Cream

Brown

Black

Tan

Dark red

Beige

Bow belle

We are dotty about the divine Miss Lumley in this spotted bow tie knit. It's the perfect outfit for those difficult restaurants that insist that one wear a tie…

MEASUREMENTS
To fit chest/bust: 87(92:97:102:107)cm
Length: 68(69:70:72:73)cm
Sleeve length: 48cm
Figures in brackets refer to the larger sizes.
Where only one figure is given this refers to all sizes.

MATERIALS
9(10:11:11) x 50g balls of 4-ply yarn in main shade – navy (A)
1 x 50g ball of 4-ply yarn in each of contrast shades – white (B), red (C)
1 pair each of 2.75mm and 3.25mm knitting needles
The quantities of yarn given are based on average requirements and are therefore approximate.

TENSION
28 sts and 36 rows to 10cm square over st st on 3.25mm needles (or size needed to obtain given tension).

ABBREVIATIONS
alt = alternate; **beg** = beginning; **cont** = continue; **dec** = decrease; **foll** = following; **inc** = increase; **K** = knit; **P** = purl; **patt** = pattern; **rem** = remaining **rep** = repeat; **RS** = right side; **st(s)** = stitch(es); **st st** = stocking stitch; **tog** = together; **WS** = wrong side.

BACK
With 2.75mm needles and main shade A, cast on 126(134:140:148:152) sts. Work in K1, P1 rib for 7cm.
Change to 3.25mm needles and starting with a K row, work in st st.
Cont straight until work measures 45(46:47:48:49)cm from beg, ending with a P row.

Shape armholes
* Cast off 6 sts at beg of next 2 rows.
Dec 1 st at both ends of the next 10 rows.
Dec 1 st. at both ends of the foll 2 alt rows. [90(98:104:112:116) sts.] *
Work straight until armhole measures 23(23:23:24:24)cm, ending with a P row.

Shape shoulders
Cast off 6(7:7:8:8) sts at beg of next 6 rows, and 4(5:7:8:9) sts at beg of next 2 rows. Leave rem 46(46:48:48:50) sts on a stitch holder.

Make pocket lining
With 3.25mm needles and B, cast on 34 sts. Starting with K row, work in st st for 10cm, ending with a K row. Leave sts on a spare needle.

FRONT
Work as given for back until work measures 42(43:44:46:47)cm from beg, ending with a P row.

CHART 1

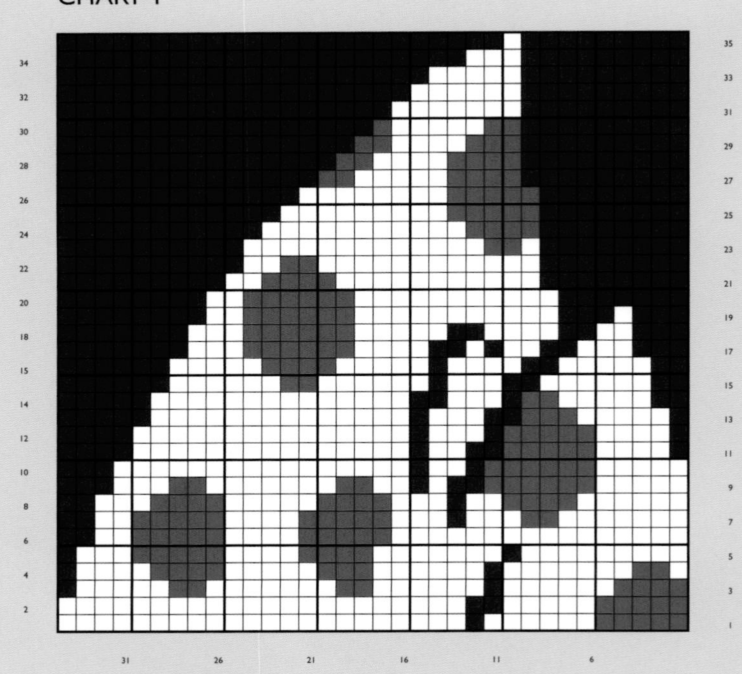

A Navy

B White

C Red

CHART 2

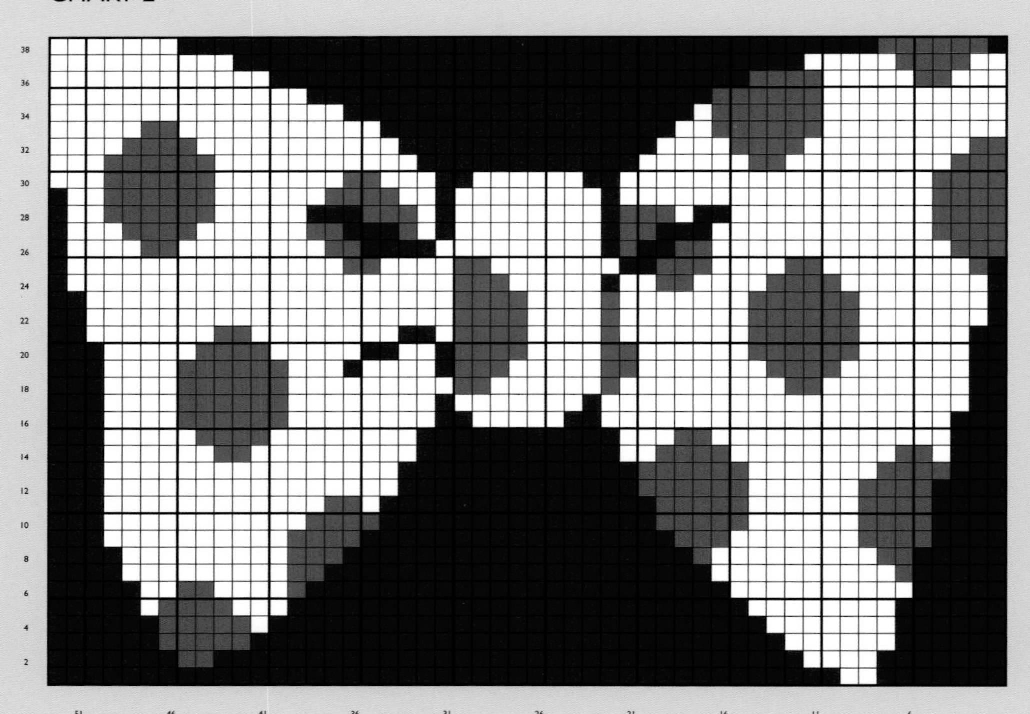

Next row: K14(16:16:20:20) sts, cast off 34 sts, K to end.
Next row: P78(84:90:94:98) sts, P across 34 sts of pocket lining, P to end of row.
Next row: K14(16:16:20:20) sts, K 1st row of patt from Chart 1, K to end of row.
Next row: P78(84:90:94:98) sts, P 2nd row of patt from Chart 1, P to end of row.
Cont working rows of patt from Chart 1 as placed.
At the same time: When work measures same as back to armholes ending with a P row, shape armholes.

Shape armholes

Work as for back from * to *.
Keeping armhole edge straight, work rem rows of Chart 1. When chart completed, work 1 row in A.
Next row: K19(23:26:30:32) sts, K 1st row of patt from Chart 2, K to end.
Next row: P19(23:26:30:32) sts, P 2nd row of patt from Chart 2, P to end.
Cont working rows of patt from Chart 2 as placed.

Shape neck

When patt rows completed and with RS of work facing, K32(36:38:42:43) sts, turn, leave rem sts on a spare needle.
** Dec 1 st at neck edge on next 6 rows and foll 4 alt rows. [22(26:28:32:33) sts.]
Work straight until length measures same as back to shoulder, ending at armhole edge.

Shape shoulders

Cast off 6(7:7:8:8) sts at beg of next and foll 2 alt rows.
Work 1 row.
Cast off 4(5:7:8:9) sts. With RS of work facing, slip next 26(26:28:28:30) sts onto a stitch holder.
Rejoin yarn to next st and K to end of row.
Complete to match first side from ** to end.

SLEEVES (both alike)

With 2.75mm needles and A, cast on 68 sts.
Work in K1, P1 rib for 8cm.
Change to 3.25mm needles and starting with a K row, work in st st.
Inc 1 st at both ends of next and every foll 6th row until there are 112 sts.
Work straight until sleeve measures 48cm or required length from beg, ending with a P row.

Shape top

Cast off 6 sts at beg next 2 rows.
Dec 1 st at both ends of the next 8 rows.
Dec 1 st at both ends of every foll alt row until there are 54 sts.
Dec 1 st at both ends of next 11 rows.
Work 1 row.
Cast off 4 sts at beg of next 6 rows.
Cast off rem 8 sts.

NECKBAND

Sew up left shoulder seam. With 2.75mm needles and A and RS of work facing, pick up and knit 46(46:48:48:50) sts from back neck, 24 sts from left side neck, 26(26:28:28:30) sts from centre front, and 24 sts from right side neck. [120(120:124:124:128) sts.]
Work in K1, P1 rib for 5cm. Cast off loosely in rib.

TO MAKE UP

Press work according to yarn instructions, omitting ribbing. Sew up right shoulder and neckband. Fold neckband in half and sew down on WS. Sew pocket lining in place.
Set in sleeves, matching centre of sleeve top to shoulder seam. Sew up side and sleeve seams.

His 'n' hers tuxedos

The tuxedo jacket found popularity in the 1880s. Rumour has it that an American chap from Tuxedo Park, a 'tony' area of upper New York state, was staying with the Prince of Wales at Sandringham in 1886. Unsure what to wear he asked the Prince for advice and was promptly sent to his personal tailor in Savile Row, where they fitted him with a new style of jacket that the Prince had taken to wearing. When he returned home to the States the jacket caught on with the upmarket crowd in his local neighbourhood and was henceforth known as the 'tuxedo'. Our his-and-hers knitted versions are being modelled by the ever stylish Vassos Alexander and Aphra Brandreth.

HIS TUXEDO

MEASUREMENTS

To fit chest/bust: 87(92:97:102:107)cm
Length: 57(58.5:61:63.5:66)cm
Sleeve length: 48.5(49.5:51:52:53.5)cm
Figures in brackets refer to the larger sizes.
Where only one figure is given this refers to all sizes.

MATERIALS

10(10:11:11:12) x 50g balls of 4-ply yarn in main shade – black (A)
1 x 50g ball of 4-ply yarn in each of contrast shades – sparkly black (B), cream (C), red (D)
Small amounts of contrast shades – dark red (E), pink (F), grey (G), gold (H), light grey (I)
1 pair each of 2.75mm and 3mm knitting needles
The quantities of yarn given are based on average requirements and are therefore approximate.

TENSION

32 sts and 40 rows to 10cm square over st st on 3mm needles (or size needed to obtain given tension).

ABBREVIATIONS

alt = alternate; **beg** = beginning; **cont** = continue; **dec** = decrease; **foll** = following; **inc** = increase; **K** = knit; **P** = purl; **patt** = pattern; **rem** = remaining **rep** = repeat; **RS** = right side; **st(s)** = stitch(es); **st st** = stocking stitch; **tog** = together; **WS** = wrong side.

FRONT

With 2.75mm needles and A, cast on 126(134:142:150:158) sts.
Work in K2, P2 rib for 4cm.
Change to 3mm needles.
Inc row: K, inc 20 sts evenly across row. [146(154:162:170:178) sts.]
Next row: P.
Work in st st until work measures 9.5(11:13.5:16:18.5)cm from cast-on edge.

Place chart

Next row: K2(6:10:14:18) sts, work 1st row of Chart 1, K to end.
Next row: P2(6:10:14:18) sts, work 2nd row of Chart 1, P to end.
Work chart as now set until Row 160.

Shape neck

Row 161: K in patt 57(61:65:69:73) sts, put rem sts onto a stitch holder.

Cont and at Rows 162 and 164 cast off 3 sts, P to end.

Rows 166, 168 and 170: Cast off 2 sts, P to end.

Beg at Row 172, dec at neck edge on each WS row 3 times. [42(46:50:54:58) sts.]

Cont working from chart until Row 190 is completed. Cast off loosely.

Return to rem sts and slip first 32 sts onto a stitch holder.

- **A** Black
- **B** Sparkly black
- **C** Cream
- **D** Red
- **E** Dark Red
- **F** Pink
- **G** Grey
- **H** Gold
- **I** Light grey

With RS facing, rejoin yarn and K to end. [57(61:65:69:73) sts.]
Work from chart and at Rows 163 and 165 cast off 3 sts, K to end.
Rows 167, 169 and 171: Cast off 2 sts, K to end.
Beg at Row 173, dec at neck edge on every RS row 3 times. [42(46:50:54:58) sts.]
Cont working from chart until Row 190 is completed. Cast off loosely.

BACK

With 2.75mm needles and A, cast on 126(134:142:150:158) sts.
Work in K2, P2 rib for 4cm.
Change to 3mm needles.
Inc row: K, inc 20 sts evenly across row. [146(154:162:170: 178) sts.]
Next row: P.
Work in st st until work measures 57(58.5:61:63.5: 66)cm.
Cast off 42(46:50:54:58) sts loosely for shoulder.
Slip 62 sts onto a stitch holder.
Cast off rem 42(46:50:54:58) sts for shoulder.

SLEEVES (both alike)

With 2.75mm needles and C, cast on 72 sts.
Work in K2, P2 rib for 2cm.
Change to A and work a further 2cm in K2, P2 rib.
Change to 3mm needles.
Inc row: K, inc 20 sts evenly across row.
Working in st st, inc 1 st at each end of foll 6th rows until there are 146(152:160:168:176) sts.
Work straight until work measures 48.5(49.5:51:52: 53.5)cm.
Cast off loosely.

NECKBAND

Join right shoulder seam.
With 2.75mm needles and C, pick up and knit 29 sts from left front neck, knit 32 sts from stitch holder, pick up and knit 29 sts up right neck edge and knit 62 sts from back neck stitch holder. [152 sts.] Work in K2, P2 rib for 6cm.
Cast off loosely.

TO MAKE UP

Join left shoulder and neckband.
Fold neckband in half and loosely slip stitch to the inside.
Measure and mark 23(24:25.5:26.5:28)cm each side of shoulder seam and sew sleeves between these marks.
Join side and sleeve seams.

HER TUXEDO

MEASUREMENTS

To fit chest/bust: 87(92:97:102:107)cm
Length: 57(58.5:61:63.5:66)cm
Sleeve length: 48.5(49.5:51:52:53.5)cm
Figures in brackets refer to the larger sizes.
Where only one figure is given this refers to all sizes.

MATERIALS

10(10:11:11:12) x 50g balls of 4-ply yarn in main shade – black (A)
1 x 50g ball of 4-ply yarn in each of contrast shades – cream (B), silver (C), sparkly pink (D), dark pink (E)
Small amounts of contrast shades – green (F), dark red (G), light pink (H), grey (I), gold (J)
1 pair each of 2.75mm and 3mm knitting needles
The quantities of yarn given are based on average requirements and are therefore approximate.

TENSION

32 sts and 40 rows to 10cm square over st st on 3mm needles (or size needed to obtain given tension).

ABBREVIATIONS

alt = alternate; **beg** = beginning; **cont** = continue; **dec** = decrease; **foll** = following; **inc** = increase; **K** = knit; **P** = purl; **patt** = pattern; **rem** = remaining **rep** = repeat; **RS** = right side; **st(s)** = stitch(es); **st st** = stocking stitch; **tog** = together; **WS** = wrong side.

FRONT

With 2.75mm needles and A, cast on 126:(134:142:150:158) sts.
Work in K2, P2 rib for 4cm.
Change to 3mm needles.
Inc row: K, inc 20 sts evenly across row. [146(154:162:170:178) sts.]
Next row: P.
Work in st st until work measures 8.5(10:12.5:15:17.5)cm from cast-on edge, ending with a WS row.

Place chart

Next row: K6(10:14:18:22) sts, work 1st row of Chart 2, K to end.
Next row: P6(10:14:18:22) sts, work 2nd row of Chart 2, P to end.
Work chart as now set until Row 164.

Shape neck

Row 165: K in patt 57(61:65:69:73) sts, put rem sts onto a stitch holder.
Cont and at Rows 166 and 168, cast off 3 sts, P to end.
Rows 170, 172 and 174: Cast off 2 sts, P to end.
Beg at Row 176, dec at neck edge on each WS row 3 times. [42(46:50:54:58) sts.]
Cont working from chart until Row 194 is completed. Cast off loosely.

Return to rem sts and slip first 32 sts onto a stitch holder.
With RS facing, rejoin yarn and K to end. [57(61:65:69:73) sts.]
Continue and at Rows 167 and 169, cast off 3 sts, K to end.
Rows 171, 173 and 175: Cast off 2 sts, K to end.
Beg at Row 177, dec at neck edge on every RS row 3 times. [42(46:50:54:58) sts.]
Cont working from chart until Row 194 is completed. Cast off loosely.

BACK

With 2.75mm needles and A, cast on 126(134:142:150:158) sts.
Work in K2, P2 rib for 4cm.
Change to 3mm needles.
Inc row: K, inc 20 sts evenly across row. [146(154:162:170:178) sts.]
Next row: P.
Work in st st until work measures 57(58.5:61:63.5:66)cm.
Cast off 42(46:50:54:58) sts loosely for shoulder.
Slip 62 sts onto a stitch holder.
Cast off rem 42(46:50:54:58) sts for shoulder.

SLEEVES (both alike)

With 2.75mm needles and A, cast on 72 sts.
Work in K2, P2 rib for 4cm.
Change to 3mm needles.
Inc row: K, inc 20 sts evenly across row.
Working in st st, inc 1 st at each end of foll 6th rows until there are 146(152:160:168:176) sts.
Work straight until work measures 48.5(49.5:51:52:53.5)cm, ending with a WS row.
Cast off loosely.

A Black	F Green
B Cream	G Dark red
C Silver	H Light pink
D Sparkly pink	I Grey
E Dark Pink	J Gold

NECKBAND

Join right shoulder seam.
With 2.75mm needles and B, pick up and knit 29 sts from left front neck, knit 32 sts from stitch holder, pick up and knit 29 sts up right neck edge and knit 62 sts from back neck stitch holder. [152 sts.]
Work in K2, P2 rib for 6cm.
Cast off loosely.

TO MAKE UP

Join left shoulder and neckband.
Fold neckband in half and loosely slip stitch to the inside.

Measure and mark 23(24:25.5:26.5:28)cm each side of shoulder seam and sew sleeves between these marks.
Join side and sleeve seams.

Sweet treat

Like our beautiful birthday cake jumper, sixties supermodel Sandra Howard is always in fashion. When Sandra's not busy modelling for Vogue (she is one of the only models to have featured on the cover of the American edition twice in a row), she's writing her bestselling novels and travelling round the world with her dapper chap, former leader of the Conservative party, Lord (Michael) Howard of Lympne. Sandra Howard in our birthday cake jumper? Now that's a recipe for success.

MEASUREMENTS

To fit chest/bust: 87(92:97:102:107)cm
Length: 57(59:61:64:66)cm
Sleeve length: 48.5(49.5:51:52:53.5)cm
Figures in brackets refer to the larger sizes.
Where only one figure is given this refers to all sizes.

MATERIALS

9(10:11:11:12) x 50g balls of 4-ply yarn in main shade – dark blue (A)
1 x 50g ball of 4-ply yarn in contrast shade – cream (B)
1 x 50g ball of 4-ply yarn in contrast shade – brown (C)
Small amounts of contrast shades – yellow (D), light blue (E), pink (F), red (G)
1 pair each of 2.75mm and 3mm knitting needles
The quantities of yarn given are based on average requirements and are therefore approximate.

TENSION

32 sts and 40 rows to 10cm square over st st on 3mm needles (or size needed to obtain given tension).

ABBREVIATIONS

alt = alternate; **beg** = beginning; **cont** = continue; **dec** = decrease; **foll** = following; **inc** = increase; **K** = knit; **P** = purl; **patt** = pattern; **rem** = remaining **rep** = repeat; **RS** = right side; **st(s)** = stitch(es); **st st** = stocking stitch; **tog** = together; **WS** = wrong side.

BACK

With 2.75mm needles and A, cast on 126(134:142:150:158) sts.
Work in K2, P2 rib for 6cm.
Change to 3mm needles.
Inc row: K inc 20 sts evenly across row. [146(154:162:170:178) sts.]
Next row: P.
Work in st st until work measures 57(58.5:61:63.5:66)cm, from cast-on edge, ending with a WS row.
Cast off 42(46:50:54:58) sts loosely for shoulder.
Slip 62 sts onto a stitch holder.
Cast off rem 42(46:50:54:58) sts for shoulder.

FRONT

With 2.75mm needles and A, cast on 126(134:142:150:158) sts.
Work in K2, P2 rib for 6cm.
Change to 3mm needles.
Inc row: K inc 20 sts evenly across row.

[146(154:162:170:178) sts.]
Next row: P.
Work in st st until work measures 15(16.5:19:21.5:24)cm from cast-on edge.

Place chart

K43(47:51:55:59) sts, work 1st row of chart, K to end.
P43(47:51:55:59) sts, work 2nd row of chart, P to end.
Work with chart as now set.
Cont in st st until work measures 49.5(51:53.5:56:58.5)cm, ending on a WS row.

Shape neck

Next row: K57(61:65:69:73) sts, put rem sts onto a stitch holder.
Next row: Cast off 3 sts, P to end.
Next row: K.
Rep last two rows one more time.
Next row: Cast off 2 sts, P to end.
Next row: K.
Rep last two rows two more times.
Dec at neck edge on each WS row 3 times.
[42(46:50:54:58) sts.]
Work 14 rows of st st.
Cast off loosely.

Return to rem stitches and slip first 32 sts onto a stitch holder.
With RS facing, rejoin yarn and K to end.
[57(61:65:69:73) sts.]
Next row: P.

- **A** Dark blue
- **B** Cream
- **C** Brown
- **D** Yellow
- **E** Light blue
- **F** Pink
- **G** Red

Next row: Cast off 3 sts, K to end.
Next row: P.
Rep last two rows one more time.
Next row: Cast off 2 sts, K to end.
Next row: P.
Rep last two rows two more times.
Dec at neck edge on every RS row 3 times.
[42(46:50:54:58) sts.]
Work 13 rows in st st.
Cast off loosely.

SLEEVES (both alike)

With 2.75mm needles and A, cast on 72 sts.
Work in K2, P2 rib for 6cm.
Change to 3mm needles.
Inc row: K, inc 20 sts evenly across row.
Working in st st, inc 1 st at each end of foll 6th rows until there are 146(152:160:168:176) sts.
Work straight until work measures 48.5(49.5:51:52:53.5)cm.
Cast off loosely.

NECKBAND

Join right shoulder seam.
With 2.75mm needles and A, pick up and knit 29 sts from left front neck, knit 32 sts from stitch holder, pick up and knit 29 sts up right neck edge and knit 62 sts from back neck stitch holder. [152 sts.]
Work in K2, P2 rib for 10cm.
Cast off loosely.

TO MAKE UP

Join left shoulder and neckband.
Fold neckband in half and loosely slip stitch to the inside.
Measure and mark 23(24:25.5:26.5:28)cm each side of shoulder seam and sew sleeves between these marks.
Join side and sleeve seams.

Heart throb

Be still my beating heart – who's that dashing chap in the delightful jumper? Why it's Mark Lyndhurst, former Coldstream Guards officer, acclaimed author of Code Black*. He's kind-hearted, big-hearted and certainly gets our hearts racing in this cute and cosy knit.*

MEASUREMENTS

To fit chest/bust: 87(92:97:102:107)cm
Length: 61(65:67:69:71)cm
Sleeve length: 49(49:50:51:51)cm
Figures in brackets refer to the larger sizes.
Where only one figure is given this refers to all sizes.

MATERIALS

8(8:9:9:10) x 50g balls of 4-ply yarn in main shade – royal blue (A)
1 x 50g ball of 4-ply yarn in contrast shade – red (B)
1 pair each of 2.75mm and 3.25mm knitting needles
The quantities of yarn given are based on average requirements and are therefore approximate.

TENSION

28 stitches and 36 rows to 10cm square over st st on 3.25mm needles (or size needed to obtain given tension).

ABBREVIATIONS

alt = alternate; **beg** = beginning; **cont** = continue; **dec** = decrease; **foll** = following; **inc** = increase; **K** = knit; **P** = purl; **patt** = pattern; **rem** = remaining; **rep** = repeat; **RS** = right side; **st(s)** = stitch(es); **st st** = stocking stitch; **tbl** = through back of loop; **tog** = together; **WS** = wrong side.

BACK

With 2.75mm needles and A, cast on 128(132:140:148:152) sts. Work in K2, P2 rib for 7cm.
Change to 3.25mm needles and starting with a K row, work in st st.
Cont straight until work measures 42(46:48:49:51) cm from beg, ending with a P row.

Shape armholes

Inc 1 st at both ends of the next and every foll 10th row, 6 times. [142(146:154:162:166) sts.]
Work 5(7:7:9:9) rows straight.

Shape shoulders

Cast off 6(6:6:7:7) sts at beg of next 14 rows and 5(6:9:6:7) sts at beg of next 2 rows.
Leave rem 48(50:52:52:54) sts on a stitch holder.

FRONT

With 2.75mm needles and A, cast on 128(132:140:148:152) sts. Work in K2, P2 rib for 7cm.
Change to 3.25mm needles and starting with a K row, work in st st.
Cont straight until work measures 17(21:23:25:27)cm from beg, ending with a P row.
Next row: K22(24:28:32:34) sts, K 1st row of patt from chart, K to end of row.

Next row: P23(25:29:33:35) sts, P 2nd row of patt from chart, P to end of row.
Cont working rows of patt from chart as placed.
At the same time: When work measures same as back to armholes, ending with a P row, shape armholes.

Shape armholes

Inc 1 st at both ends of next and every foll 10th row, 6 times.
At the same time: When work measures 56(60:62:64:66)cm from beg, shape neck.

Shape neck

With RS of work facing, K57(59:62:66:67) sts, turn, leave rem sts on a spare needle.
* Dec 1 st at neck edge on next 12 rows.
Work straight until length measures same as back to shoulder, ending at armhole edge.

Shape shoulders

Cast off 6(6:6:7:7) sts at beg of next and foll 6 alt rows.
Work 1 row. Cast off 5(6:9:6:7) sts.
With RS of work facing, slip next 24(26:28:28:30) sts onto a stitch holder.
Rejoin yarn to next st and K to end of row.
Complete to match first side from * to end.

SLEEVES (both alike)

With 2.75mm needles and A, cast on 64(64:68:68:72) sts. Work in K2, P2 rib for 8cm.
On the last row inc 48(48:48:52:52) sts evenly.
[112(112:116:120:124) sts.]
Change to 3.25mm needles and starting with a K row, work in st st.
Cont straight until work measures 49(49:50:51:51)cm from beg.
Cast off.

NECKBAND

Sew up left shoulder seam.
With 2.75mm needles and RS of work facing, pick up and knit 48(50:52:52:54) sts from back neck, 24 sts from left side neck, 24(26:28:28:30 sts from centre front and 24 sts from right side neck.
[120(124:128:128:132) sts.]
Work in K2, P2 rib for 5cm. Cast off loosely in rib.

TO MAKE UP

Press work according to yarn instructions, omitting ribbing. Sew up right shoulder and neckband. Fold neckband in half and sew down on WS. Sew in sleeves. Sew up side and sleeve seams.

A Royal Blue
B Red

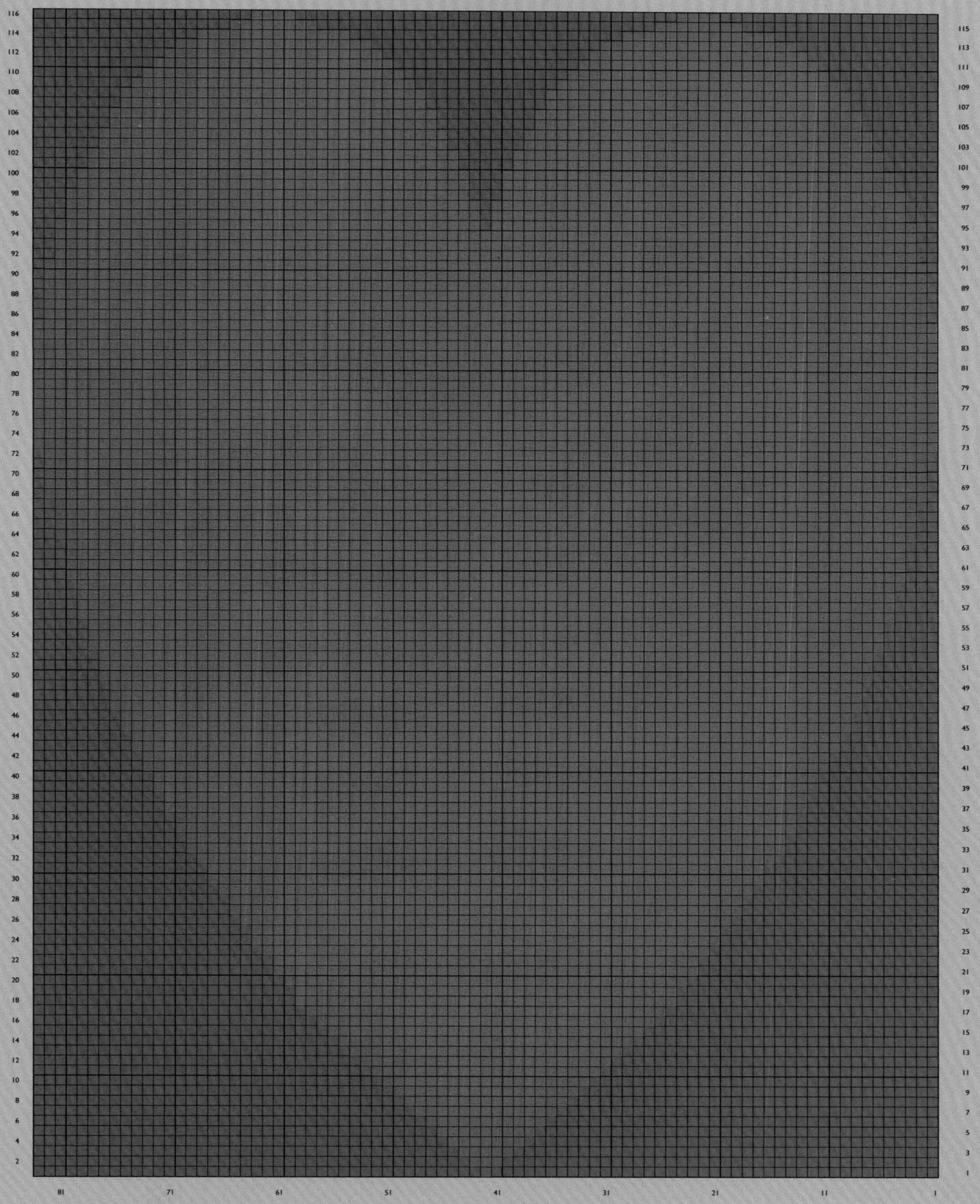

116 114 112 110 108 106 104 102 100 98 96 94 92 90 88 86 84 82 80 78 76 74 72 70 68 66 64 62 60 58 56 54 52 50 48 46 44 42 40 38 36 34 32 30 28 26 24 22 20 18 16 14 12 10 8 6 4 2

115 113 111 109 107 105 103 101 99 97 95 93 91 89 87 85 83 81 79 77 75 73 71 69 67 65 63 61 59 57 55 53 51 49 47 45 43 41 39 37 35 33 31 29 27 25 23 21 19 17 15 13 11 9 7 5 3 1

81 71 61 51 41 31 21 11 1

Rib tickling

Jake Spark looks spooktacular in this original Linda O'Brien design. This jumper isn't just for Halloween, Jake always wears it when he's out on the town with one of his ghoul-friends.

MEASUREMENTS

To fit chest/bust: 82(87:92:97:102)cm
Length: 48(52:56:60:64)cm
Sleeve length: 46.5(48.5:49.5:51:52)cm
Figures in brackets refer to the larger sizes.
Where only one figure is given this refers to all sizes.

MATERIALS

7(8:9:9:10) x 50g balls of DK yarn in main shade – black (A)
4(4:4:4:5) x 50g balls of DK yarn in contrast shade – cream (B)
1 pair each of 3.25mm and 4mm knitting needles
The quantities of yarn given are based on average requirements and are therefore approximate.

TENSION

22 stitches and 30 rows to 10cm square over st st on 4mm needles (or size needed to obtain given tension).

ABBREVIATIONS

alt = alternate; beg = beginning; cont = continue; dec = decrease; foll = following; inc = increase; K = knit; P = purl; patt = pattern; rem = remaining; rep = repeat; RS = right side; st(s) = stitch(es); st st = stocking stitch; tbl = through back of loop; tog = together; WS = wrong side.

FRONT

With 3.25mm needles and A, cast on 80(84:88:92:96) sts and work in K1, P1 rib for 16 rows.
Change to 4mm needles.
Inc row: K across, inc 14(16:18:20:22) sts evenly across row. [94(100:106:112:118) sts.]
Next row: P.

Place chart

Next row: K0(3:6:9:12) then, working in st st, work 1st row of Chart 1, K0(3:6:9:12).
Next row: P0(3:6:9:12) then work 2nd row of Chart 1, P0(3:6:9:12).
Work the first 12 rows of the chart as now set, then rep them 0(1:2:3:4) times more. [12(24:36:48:60) patt rows worked.] **
Now starting with the 13th row, work from chart as set until 114th row of chart has been completed, thus ending with a WS row.

Shape front neck

Next row (row 115 of chart): Knit in patt 40(43:46:49:52) sts, turn and cont on this first set of sts only, placing rem sts onto a stitch holder.
*** Keeping chart correct, dec 1 st at neck edge on every row until 30(33:36:39:42) sts rem.
Now cont straight, changing to B at Row 128 for sts outside the chart, until chart is complete (134th row worked).

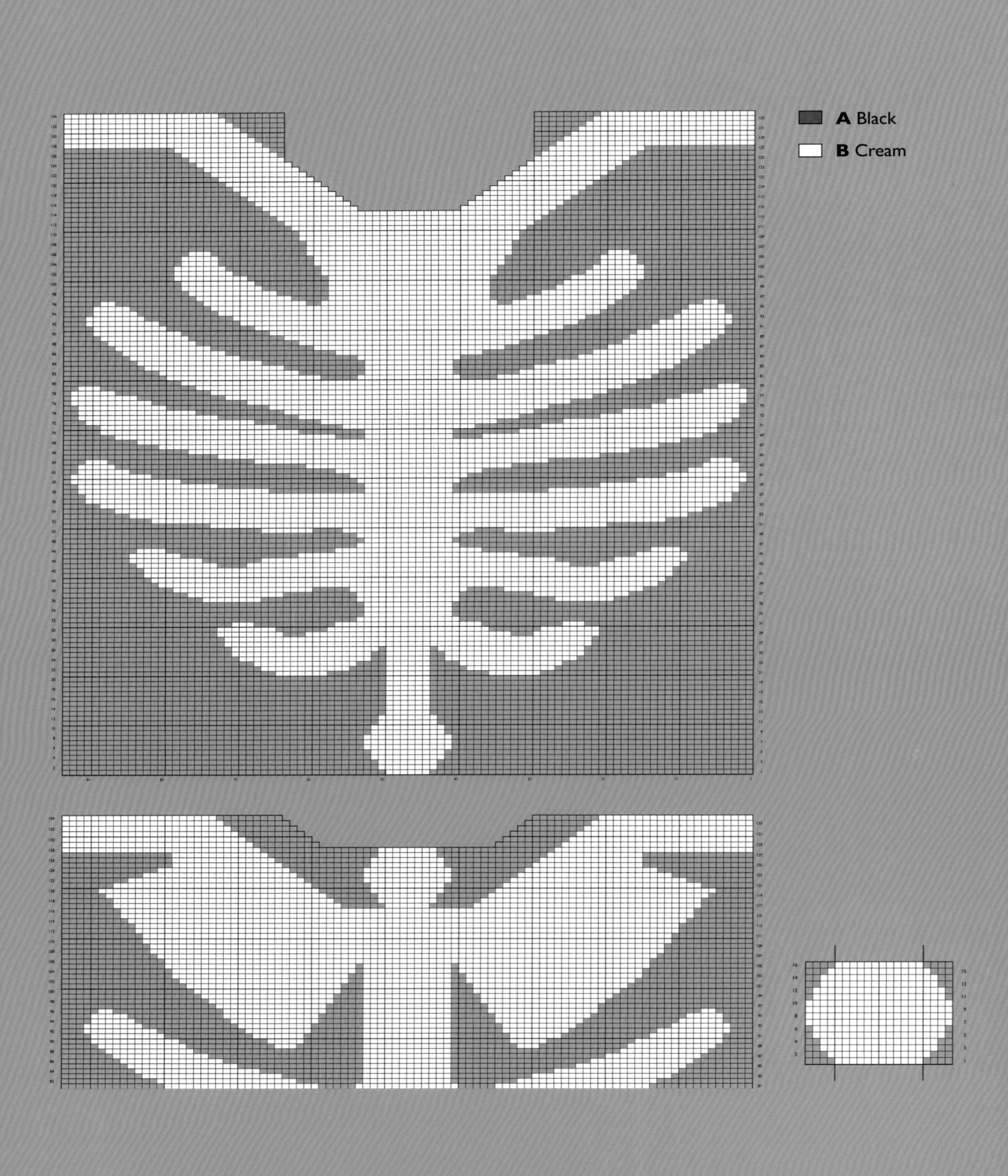
A Black
B Cream

Cast off all sts fairly loosely.
Return to rem sts and slip first 14 sts onto a stitch holder.
With RS facing, rejoin yarn to rem sts and patt to end of row.
Now work as for first side from *** to end.

BACK

Work as for front to **.
Now starting with the 13th row, work from Chart 1 as set until the 80th row of chart has been completed, thus ending with a WS row.
Now starting with the 81st row, work from Chart 2, keeping patt as set.
Cont until 128th row of chart has been worked, changing to B at Row 128 for stitches outside the chart, thus ending with a WS row.

Shape back neck

Next row (row 129 of chart): Patt 35(38:41:44:47) sts, turn and cont on this first set of sts only, placing rem sts onto a stitch holder.
**** Keeping chart correct, dec 1 st at neck edge on next 5 rows (134th row of chart complete.)
Cast off rem 30(33:36:39:42) sts fairly loosely
Return to rem sts and slip first 24 sts onto a stitch holder. With RS facing, rejoin yarn to rem sts and patt to end of row.
Now work as for first side from **** to end.

SLEEVES (both alike)

With 3.25mm needles and A, cast on 46(48:50:52:54) sts and work in K1, P1 rib for 16 rows.
Change to 4mm needles.
Inc row: K across, inc 20 sts evenly across row. [66(68:70:72:74) sts.]
Next row: P.

Place chart

Row 1 (RS facing): K27(28:29:30:31) in A, K12 in B, K to end in A.
Cont in st st and patt as now set, keeping the centre 12 sts in B straight.
At the same time: Inc 1 st at each end of 5th row and then every foll 6th row until work measures 18(19:20.5:21.5:23)cm, ending with a WS row, and working inc sts into A at either side.
Still keeping inc as before, work Chart 3 as shown.
Cont in the 12-st patt as before, and inc as before, until there are 94(100:104:110:114) sts on the needle.
Now work straight in st st and in patt until the sleeve measures 46.5(48.5:49.5:51:52)cm from cast on edge, ending with a WS row.
Cast off sts fairly loosely.

NECKBAND

Join right shoulder seam, matching patt.
With 3.25mm needles and A and RS facing, pick up and knit 18 sts down left front neck, K14 sts from stitch holder, pick up and knit 18 sts up right front neck and 5 sts down right back neck, K24 sts from stitch holder and finally pick up and knit 5 sts up left back neck. [84 sts.]
Work in K1, P1 rib for 12 rows.
Cast off fairly loosely ribwise.

TO MAKE UP

Join left shoulder and neckband.
Measure and mark 21(22.5:23.5:25:26)cm each side of shoulder seam and sew sleeves between these marks, matching patt.
Join side and sleeve seams, matching patt at the shoulders.

Friendly ghost

This jumper is a spooky favourite that works all year round. It's destined to be a fashion sensation from ghost to ghost. Luckily, the little chap on the front of this updated Linda O'Brien design is super friendly, just like the lovely Martha Harlan who is modelling it for us.

MEASUREMENTS

To fit chest/bust: 87(92:97:102:107)cm
Length: 54(55:58:60:62)cm
Sleeve length: 49(51:51:52:52)cm
Figures in brackets refer to the larger sizes.
Where only one figure is given this refers to all sizes.

MATERIALS

8(8:9:10:11) x 50g balls of DK yarn in main shade – charcoal grey (A)
1 x 50g ball of DK yarn ball in contrast shade – white (B)
Small amount of black yarn to embroider smile
1 pair each of 3.25mm and 4mm knitting needles
2 small black beads or buttons for eyes
The quantities of yarn given are based on average requirements and are therefore approximate

TENSION

22 stitches and 28 rows to 10cm square over st st on 4mm needles (or size needed to obtain given tension).

ABBREVIATIONS

alt = alternate; **beg** = beginning; **cont** = continue; **dec** = decrease; **foll** = following; **inc** = increase; **K** = knit; **P** = purl; **patt** = pattern; **rem** = remaining **rep** = repeat; **RS** = right side; **st(s)** = stitch(es); **st st** = stocking stitch; **tog** = together; **WS** = wrong side.

BACK

With 3.25mm needles and A, cast on 92(96:100:104:108) sts and work in K1, P1 rib for 18 rows.
Change to 4mm needles.
Inc row: K, inc 10(12:14:16:18) sts evenly across row. [102(108:114:120:126) sts.]
Next row: P. **
Now starting with a K row, work straight in st st in A until back measures 53(54:57:59:61)cm from cast-on edge, ending with a WS row.

Shape back neck

Next row: K39(41:44:46:49) sts, turn and cont on this first set of sts only, placing rem sts onto a stitch holder.
*** Dec 1 st at neck edge on next 3 rows.
Cast off rem 36(38:41:43:46) sts fairly loosely.
Return to rem sts and slip first 26 sts onto a stitch holder. With RS facing, rejoin yarn to rem sts and K to end of row.
Now work as for first side from *** to end.

FRONT

Work as for back to **.
Work straight in st st for 2(3:4:5:6)cm ending on a WS row.

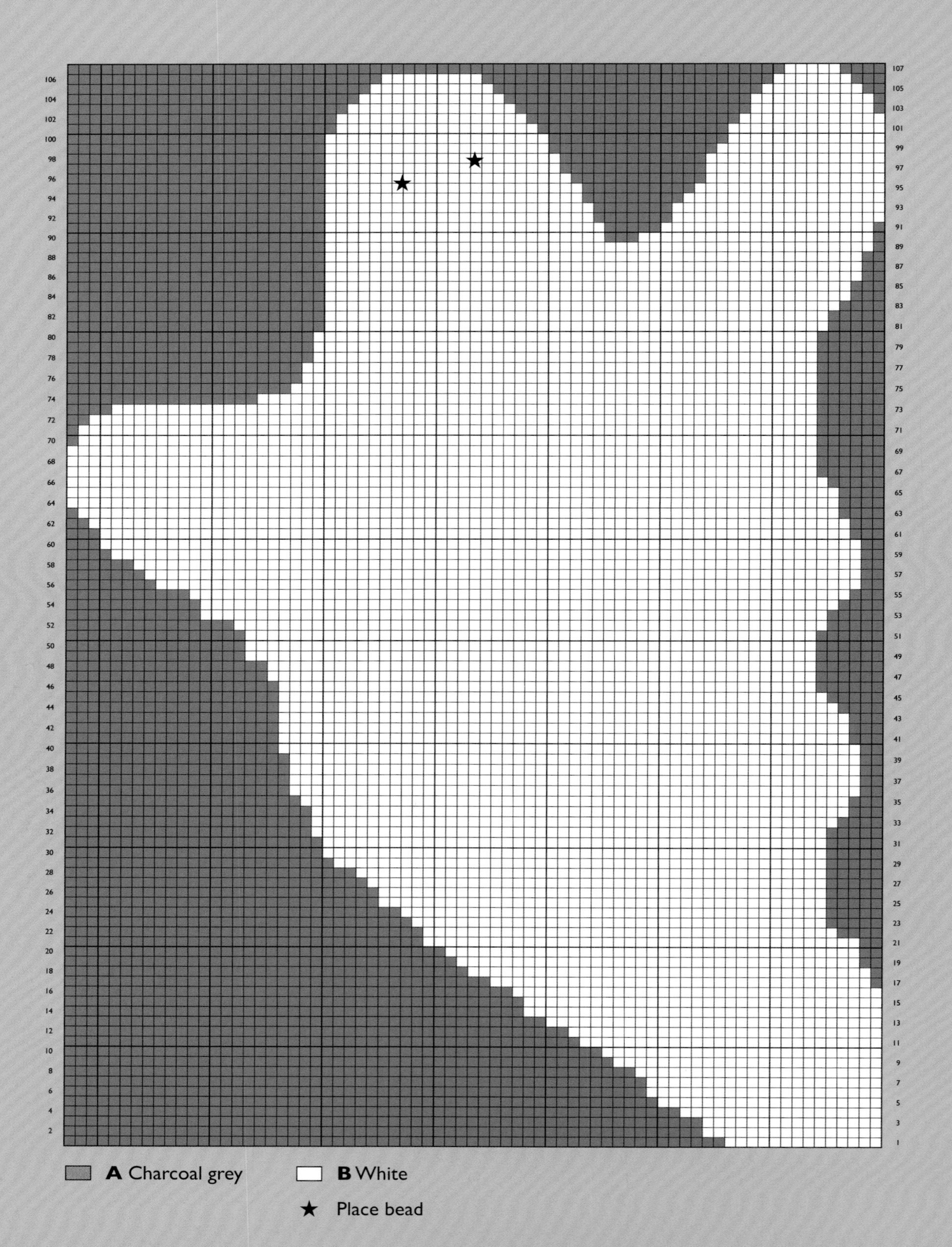
A Charcoal grey
B White
★ Place bead

Place chart

Next row: K14(17:20:23:26) sts, K 1st row of chart, K to end.
Next row: P15(18:21:24:27) sts, P 2nd row of chart, P to end.
Cont in st st with chart as placed.
When chart complete, work straight in st st in A only until front measures 48(49:52:54:56)cm from cast-on edge, ending with a WS row.

Shape front neck

Next row: K44(46:49:51:54) sts, turn and cont on this first set of sts only, placing rem sts on a stitch holder.
**** Dec 1 st at neck edge on every row until 36(38:41:43:46) sts remain. Now cont straight in st st until front measures the same as back to shoulder cast-off edge, ending with a WS row. Cast off all sts fairly loosely. Return to rem sts and slip first 16 sts onto stitch holder, with RS facing rejoin yarn to rem sts and K to end of row. Work as for first side from **** to end.

SLEEVES (both alike)

With 3.25mm needles and A, cast on 56(56:60:60:60) sts and work in K1, P1 rib for 18 rows.
Change to 4mm needles.
Increase row: K inc 24(24:30:30:34) sts across row. [80(80:90:90:94) sts.]
Now starting with a P row, cont in st st in A.
At the same time: Inc 1 st at each end of every foll 6th row until there are 100(108:116:122:126) sts on the needle.
Now cont straight in st st until sleeve measures 49(51:51:52:52)cm from cast-on edge, ending with a WS row.
Cast off all sts fairly loosely.

NECKBAND

Join right shoulder seam. With 3.25mm needles and A and RS facing, pick up and knit 17 sts down left front neck, knit 16 sts from stitch holder, pick up and knit 17 sts up right front neck, knit 4 sts down right back neck, knit 26 sts from stitch holder, and finally pick up and knit 4 sts up left back neck. [76 sts.]
Work in K1, P1 rib for 12 rows.
Cast off fairly loosely ribwise.

TO MAKE UP

Press according to ball band instructions.
Join left shoulder and neckband seam. Fold neckband in half to inside and slip stitch loosely in position. Measure and mark 23(24:25:26:27)cm each side of shoulder seam and sew sleeves between these marks. Embroider the ghost's smile with black yarn and sew on beads or buttons for eyes as in picture. Join side and sleeve seams.

Spellbound

Hubble, bubble, toil and, oh look, here comes trouble in the shape of the fabulously funny Shappi Khorsandi. If you want to look just as bewitching, get busy knitting and magic up your own version of this Linda O'Brien design.

MEASUREMENTS
To fit chest/bust: 87(92:97:102:107)cm
Length: 63(65:67:69:71)cm
Sleeve length: 49(49:50:50:51)cm
Figures in brackets refer to the larger sizes.
Where only one figure is given this refers to all sizes.

MATERIALS
8(9:9:10:10) x 50g balls of DK yarn in main shade – grey (A)
1 x 50g ball of DK yarn in each of contrast shades – white (B), red (C), black (D) and yellow (E)
1 pair each of 3.25mm and 4mm knitting needles
8–10 yellow star buttons and 3 black beads or buttons
1 medium-sized crochet hook
The quantities of yarn given are based on average requirements and are therefore approximate.

TENSION
22 stitches and 28 rows to 10cm square over st st on 4mm needles (or size needed to obtain given tension).

ABBREVIATIONS
alt = alternate; **beg** = beginning; **cont** = continue; **dec** = decrease; **foll** = following; **inc** = increase; **K** = knit; **P** = purl; **patt** = pattern; **rem** = remaining; **rep** = repeat; **RS** = right side; **st(s)** = stitch(es); **st st** = stocking stitch; **tog** = together; **WS** = wrong side.

NOTE
The line showing the rim of the cauldron, worked in D, may be embroidered or swiss-darned when work is complete rather than knitted, if preferred.

BACK
With 3.25mm needles and A, cast on 88(94:100:106:112) sts and work in K1, P1 rib for 18 rows.
Change to 4mm needles.
Inc row: K, inc 12(14:16:18:20) sts evenly across row. [100(108:116:124:132) sts.]
Next row: P. **
Now starting with a K row, work straight in st st in A until back measures 62(64:66:68:70)cm from cast-on edge, ending with a WS row.

Shape back neck
Next row: K37(41:45:49:53) sts, turn and cont on this first set of sts only, placing rem sts on a stitch holder.
*** Dec 1 st at neck edge on next 3 rows.
Cast off rem 34(38:42:46:50) sts fairly loosely.
Return to rem sts and slip first 26 sts onto a stitch holder. With RS facing, rejoin yarn to rem sts and K to end of row.
Now work as for first side from *** to end.

FRONT

Work as for back to **.
Now starting with a K row, work straight in st st in A for 46(48:50:52:54) rows, thus ending with a WS row.

Place chart

Next row: K19(23:27:31:35) in A, now work across the 62 sts from 1st row of chart, K to end.
Next row: P19(23:27:31:35), P 2nd row of chart, P to end.
The chart is now set. Cont to follow chart until the 90 rows of chart are worked.
Now work straight in A until front measures 57(59:61:63:65)cm from cast-on edge, ending with a WS row.

Shape front neck

Next row: K43(47:51:55:59) sts, turn and cont on this first set of sts only, placing rem sts onto a stitch holder.
**** Dec 1 st at neck edge on every row until 34(38:42:46:50) sts remain.
Now cont straight in st st until front measures the same as back to shoulder cast-off edge, ending with a WS row.
Cast off all sts fairly loosely.
Return to rem sts and slip first 14 sts onto a stitch holder. With RS facing rejoin yarn to rem sts and K to end of row.
Now work as for first side from **** to end.

SLEEVES (both alike)

With 3.25mm needles and A, cast on 40(44:48:52:56) sts and work in K1, P1 rib for 18 rows.
Change to 4mm needles.
Inc row: K, inc 14(16:18:20:22) sts evenly across row. [54(60:66:72:78) sts.]
Now starting with a P row, cont in st st in A.
At the same time: Inc 1 st at each end of every foll 6th row until there are 92(98:104:110:116) sts on the needle.
Now cont straight in st st until sleeve measures 49(49:50:50:51)cm from cast-on edge, ending with a WS row.
Cast off all sts fairly loosely.

NECKBAND

Join right shoulder seam. With 3.25mm needles and A and RS facing, pick up and knit 18 sts down left front neck, knit 14 sts from stitch holder, pick up and knit 18 sts up right front neck, knit 4 sts down right back neck, knit 26 sts from stitch holder and finally pick up and knit 4 sts up left back neck. [84 sts.]
Work in K1, P1 rib for 12 rows.
Cast off fairly loosely ribwise.

TO MAKE UP

Press according to ball band instructions.
Join left shoulder and neckband seam. Fold neckband in half to inside and slip stitch loosely in position. Measure and mark 23(24:25:26:27)cm each side of shoulder seam and sew sleeves between these marks.
Sew on black beads or buttons for witch's and snake's eyes.
With D embroider witch's smile, spider's legs and thread, and bat's eyes.
With E embroider spider's eyes, then make hair with strands of E looped through with a crochet hook.
Sew on stars, using the picture as a guide.

90
88
86
84
82
80
78
76
74
72
70
68
66
64
62
60
58
56
54
52
50
48
46
44
42
40
38
36
34
32
30
28
26
24
22
20
18
16
14
12
10
8
6
4
2
89
87
85
83
81
79
77
75
73
71
69
67
65
63
61
59
57
55
53
51
49
47
45
43
41
39
37
35
33
31
29
27
25
23
21
19
17
15
13
11
9
7
5
3
1

Feeling frosty

We couldn't think of anyone more appropriate to model this jumper than our very own snowman, Captain Martin Hewitt. Not only has Martin trekked to the North Pole with HRH Prince Harry and led the Walking with the Wounded team that scaled Mount Everest, he's also raced the International Paralympic circuit, culminating in representing Great Britain in the World Championships. This super cute knit will keep him cosy after a day out in icy condition; it always raises a smile and warms the cockles.

MEASUREMENTS

To fit chest/bust: 87(92:97:102:107)cm
Length: 57(58.5:61:63.5:66)cm
Sleeve length: 46.5(48.5:49.5:51:52)cm
Figures in brackets refer to the larger sizes.
Where only one figure is given this refers to all sizes.

MATERIALS

2(2:2:3:3) x 50g balls of DK yarn in dark blue (A)
2 x 50g balls of DK yarn in white (B)
9(10:10:11:11) x 50g balls of DK yarn in light blue (C)
1 x 50g ball of DK yarn in red (D)
Beads or buttons for eyes, nose and mouth
Pompom for hat
1 pair each of 3.25mm and 4mm knitting needles
The quantities of yarn given are based on average requirements and are therefore approximate.

TENSION

22 stitches and 30 rows to 10cm square over st st on 4mm needles (or size needed to obtain given tension).

ABBREVIATIONS

cont = continue; **dec** = decrease; **foll** = following; **inc** = increase; **K** = knit; **P** = purl; **patt** = pattern; **rem** = remaining; **rep** = repeat; **RS** = right side; **st(s)** = stitch(es); **st st** = stocking stitch; **WS** = wrong side.

FRONT

With 3.25mm needles and A, cast on 80(84:88:92:96) sts. Work in K1, P1 rib for 5cm. Change to 4mm needles.
Inc row: K14(16:18:20:22) sts evenly across row. [94(100:106:112:118) sts.]
Next row: P.
Work in st st for 0(1:2:3:4)cm. *

Place chart

Next row: K3(6:9:12:15) sts, working in st st, K 1st row of patt from chart, K to end.
Next row: P3(6:9:12:15) sts, then work 2nd row of patt from chart, P to end.
Cont working rows of patt from chart, changing to B for outside stitches at Row 55, and to C at row 75.
Cont in st st until work measures 50.5(52:54.5:57:59.5)cm, ending with a WS row.

Shape front neck

Next row: K40(43:46:49:52) sts, turn and cont on this first set of sts only, placing rem sts onto a stitch holder.
** Dec 1 st at neck edge on every row until 30(33:36:39:42) sts rem. Now cont straight until work measures 57(58.5:61:63.5:66)cm.

Skiing

Cast off all sts fairly loosely.
Return to rem sts and slip first 14 sts onto a stitch holder. With RS facing, rejoin yarn to rem sts and K to end of row. Now work as for first side from ** to end.

BACK

Work as for front to *.
Work in st st until work measures 24(25:26:27:28)cm.
Change to B. Work in st st until work measures 30.5(31.5:32.5:33.5:34.5)cm.
Change to C. Work in st st until work measures 55.5(57:59.5:62:64.5)cm, ending with a WS row.

Shape back neck

Next row: K35(38:41:44:47) sts, turn and cont on this first set of sts only, placing rem sts onto a stitch holder.
*** Dec 1 st at neck edge on next 4 rows.
Cast off rem 30(33:36:39:42) sts fairly loosely.
Return to rem sts and slip first 24 sts onto a stitch holder. With RS facing, rejoin yarn to rem sts and patt to end of row.
Now work as for first side from *** to end.

SLEEVES (both alike)

With 3.25mm needles and C, cast on 46(48:50:52:54) sts and work in K1, P1 rib for 5cm.
Change to 4mm needles.
Inc row: K, inc 20 sts evenly across row. [66(68:70:72:74) sts.]
Next row: P.
Cont in st st and inc 1 st at each end of 5th row and then every foll 6th row until there are 94(100:104:110:114) sts on the needle.
Now work straight in st st until sleeve measures 46.5(48.5:49.5:51:52)cm from cast-on edge, ending with a WS row.
Cast off sts fairly loosely.

NECKBAND

Join right shoulder seam.
With 3.25mm needles and A and RS facing, pick up and knit 18 sts down left front neck, knit 14 sts from stitch holder, pick up and knit 18 sts up right front neck and 5 sts down right back neck, knit 24 sts from stitch holder and finally pick up and knit 5 sts up left back neck. [84 sts.]
Work in K1, P1 rib for 2.5cm.
Cast off fairly loosely ribwise.

TO MAKE UP

Embroider chain stitch around snowman, scarf and hat as shown on chart. Using a crochet hook, knot yarn D through sts at ends of the scarf for tassels. Sew on beads for face, and pompom for hat, placing as shown on chart. Join left shoulder and neckband. Measure and mark 22(23:24:25.5:26.5)cm each side of shoulder seam and sew sleeves between these marks. Join side and sleeve seams, matching pattern at sides.

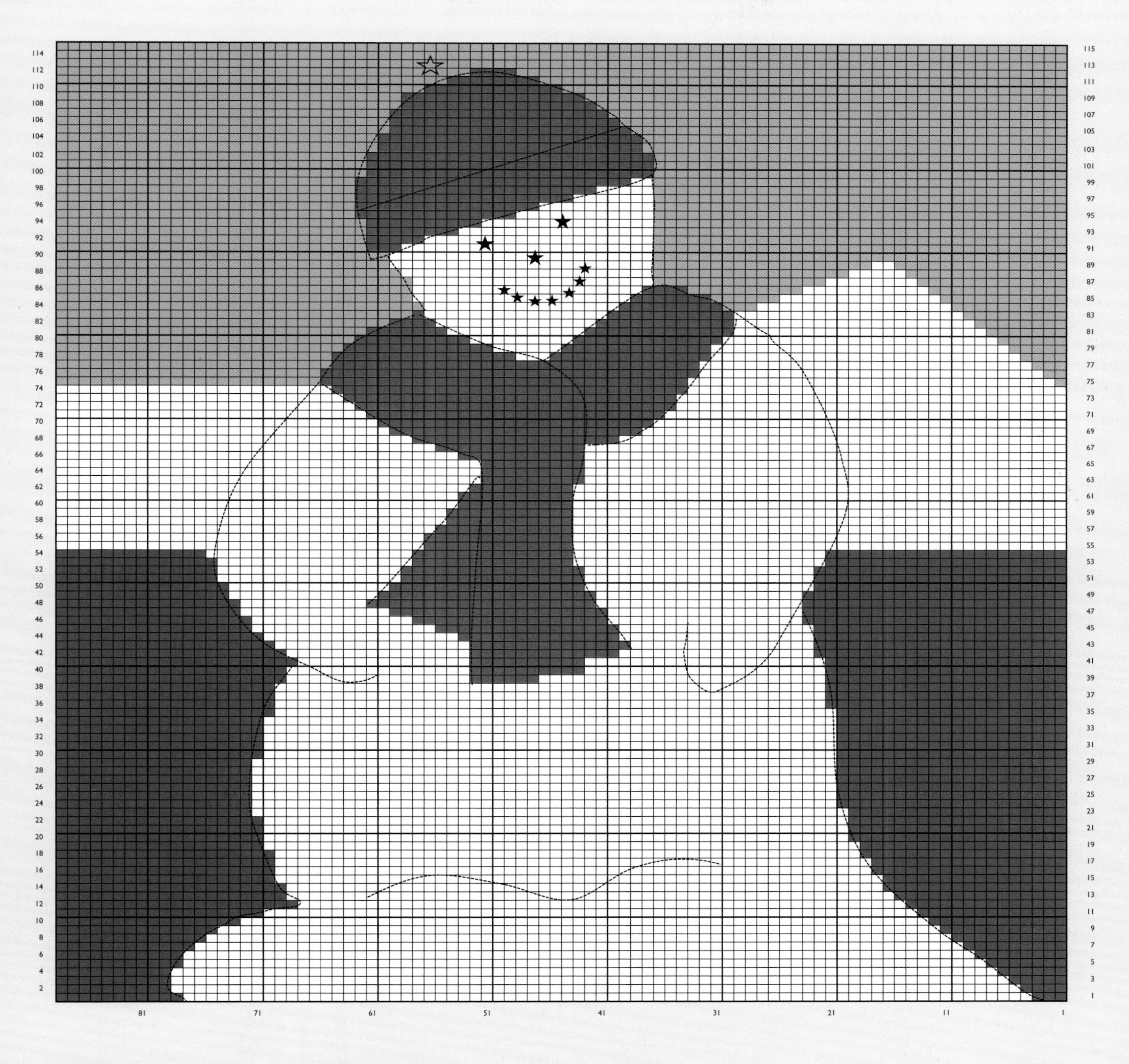

A Dark blue
B White
C Light blue
D Red
--- Chain stitch
★ Place bead
☆ Place pompom

O Christmas tree

'Tis the season to be jolly. And it looks like Peter Ginn from BBC2's Victorian Farm *series might have had a little too much festive cheer! Luckily for him he is modelling our divine Christmas tree jumper, which is guaranteed to lift anyone's spirits.*

MEASUREMENTS

To fit chest/bust: 87(92:97:102:107)cm
Length: 62(64.5:66:68.5:71)cm
Sleeve length: 48.5(49.5:51:52:53.5)cm
Figures in brackets refer to the larger sizes.
Where only one figure is given this refers to all sizes.

MATERIALS

9(10:11:11:12) x 50g balls of 4-ply yarn in main shade – cream (A)
1 x 50g ball of 4-ply yarn in contrast shade – green (B)
1 x 50g ball of 4-ply yarn in contrast shade – red (C)
Small amounts of contrast shades – gold (D) and yellow (E)
Small amounts of coloured metallic yarn for tinsel and candleholders
1 pair each of 2.75mm and 3mm knitting needles
The quantities of yarn given are based on average requirements and are therefore approximate.

TENSION

32 sts and 40 rows to 10cm square over st st on 3mm needles (or size needed to obtain given tension).

ABBREVIATIONS

alt = alternate; **beg** = beginning; **cont** = continu(e) ing; **dec** = decrease; **foll** = following; **inc** = increase; **K** = knit; **P** = purl; **patt** = pattern; **rem** = remaining **rep** = repeat; **RS** = right side; **st(s)** = stitch(es); **st st** = stocking stitch; **tog** = together; **WS** = wrong side.

FRONT

With 2.75mm needles and A, cast on 126(134:142:150:158) sts.
Work in K2, P2 rib for 5cm.
Change to 3mm needles.
Inc row: K, inc 20 sts evenly across the row. [146(154:162:170:178) sts.]
Next row: P.

Place Chart 2 (*chart is placed twice across row*)
Next row: K18(20:22:24:26) sts, work 1st row of Chart 2, K30(34:38:42:46) sts, work 1st row of Chart 2, K to end.
Next row: P18(20:22:24:26) sts, work 2nd row of Chart 2, P30(34:38:42:46) sts, work 2nd row of Chart 2, P to end.
With charts as now set, work in st st until charts are complete and work measures 13(15.5:18:20.5:23)cm, ending on a WS row.

CHART 1

Place Chart 1

Next row: K118(126:134:142:150) sts, work 1st row of Chart 1, K to end.

Next row: P118(126:134:142:150) sts, work 2nd row of Chart 1, P to end.

Work chart as now set.

Cont in st st until work measures 54.5(57:58.5:61:63.5)cm, ending on a WS row.

Shape neck

Next row: K57(61:65:69:73) sts, put rem sts onto a stitch holder.

Next row: Cast off 3 sts, P to end.

Next row: K.

Rep last two rows one more time.

Next row: Cast off 2 sts, P to end.

Next row: K.

Rep last two rows two more times.

Dec at neck edge on each WS row 3 times. [42(46:50:54:58) sts.]

Work 14 rows of st st.

Cast off loosely.

A Cream

B Green

C Red

D Gold

E Yellow

Sparkly colours for tinsel

CHART 2

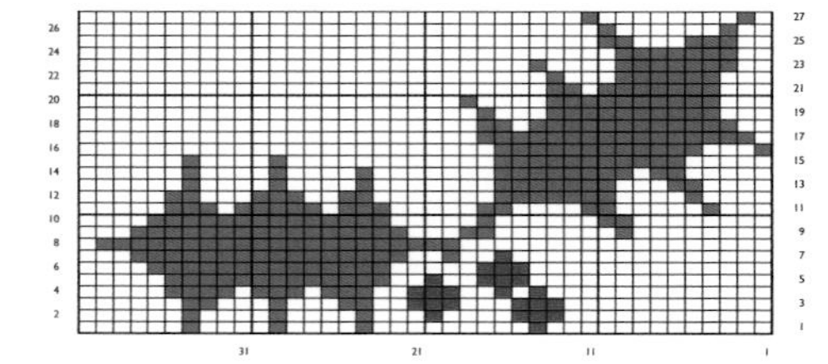

Return to rem sts and slip first 32 sts onto a stitch holder.
With RS facing, rejoin yarn and K to end. [57(61:65:69:73) sts.]
Next row: P.
Next row: Cast off 3 sts, K to end.
Next row: P.
Rep last two rows one more time.
Next row: Cast off 2 sts, K to end.
Next row: P.
Rep last two rows two more times.
Dec at neck edge on every RS row 3 times. [42(46:50:54:58) sts.]
Work 13 rows of st st.
Cast off loosely.

BACK

With 2.75mm needles and A, cast on 126(134:142:150:158) sts.
Work in K2, P2 rib for 5cm.
Change to 3mm needles.
Inc row: K, inc 20 sts evenly across row. [146(154:162:170:178) sts.]
Next row: P.

Place Chart 2 (*chart is placed twice across row*)

Next row: K18(20:22:24:26) sts, work 1st row of Chart 2, K30(34:38:42:46) sts, work 1st row of Chart 2, K to end.
Next row: P18(20:22:24:26) sts, work 2nd row of Chart 2, P30(34:38:42:46) sts, work 2nd row of Chart 2, P to end.
Complete charts as set and cont in st st until work measures 62(64.5:66:68.5:71)cm, ending on a WS row.

Shape shoulder

Cast off 42(46:50:54:58) sts loosely for shoulder, knit until there are 62 sts on right needle and slip onto a stitch holder.
Cast off rem 42(46:50:54:58) sts for shoulder.

SLEEVES (both alike)

With 2.75mm needles and A, cast on 72 sts.
Work in K2, P2 rib for 5cm.
Change to 3mm needles.
Inc row: K, inc 20 sts evenly across row.
Cont in st st, inc 1 st at each end of following 6th rows until there are 146(152:160:168:176) sts.
At the same time: When work measures 7cm, place Chart 2 in centre of sleeve and work, cont to inc outside chart as necessary.
Work straight until work measures 48.5(49.5:51:52:53.5)cm.
Cast off loosely.

NECKBAND

Join right shoulder seam.
With 2.75mm needles and A, pick up and knit 29 sts from left front neck, knit 32 sts from stitch holder, pick up and knit 29 sts up right neck edge and knit 62 sts from back neck stitch holder. [152 sts.]
Work in K2, P2 rib for 8cm.
Cast off loosely.

TO MAKE UP

Join left shoulder and neckband.
Fold neckband in half and loosely slip stitch to the inside.
Measure and mark 23(24:25.5:26.5:28)cm each side of shoulder seam and sew sleeves between these marks.
Join side and sleeve seams.

Old Saint Nick

The ideal Christmas gift? Matt Baker all wrapped up in this Father Christmas jumper. Former Blue Peter presenter, co-host of Countryfile *and* The One Show, *Matt is light-footed (he was a finalist on* Strictly Come Dancing*), quick-witted (he has won two BAFTAS for his presenting work) and kind-hearted (he raised a staggering £1.7 million for Children in Need in 2011). Matt is passionate about the countryside. He grew up on a sheep farm on the Dales, making him a natural fit for woolly knits. The sight of him in this Santa Claus sweater designed by Sarah Kim fills us with festive cheer.*

MEASUREMENTS

To fit chest/bust: 81(86:91:97:102:107:112)cm
Length: 62(63:65:67:69:71:73)cm
Sleeve length: 46(46:46:46:47:47:48)cm
Figures in brackets refer to the larger sizes.
Where only one figure is given this refers to all sizes.

MATERIALS

6(6:7:7:8:8:9) x 50g balls of DK yarn in main shade – red (MC)
1 x 50g ball of DK yarn in contrast shades – white (A)
Small amounts of DK yarn in contrast shades – black (B) and pale pink (C)
1 pair each of 3.25mm and 4mm knitting needles
4 stitch holders
2 stitch markers
The quantities of yarn given are based on average requirements and are therefore approximate.

TENSION

22 stitches and 28 rows to 10cm square over st st on 4mm needles (or size needed to obtain given tension).

ABBREVIATIONS

alt = alternate; **beg** = beginning; **cont** = continue; **dec** = decrease; **foll** = following; **inc** = increase; **K** = knit; **K2tog** = knit 2 together; **P** = purl; **P2tog** = purl 2 together; **patt** = pattern; **pm** = place marker; **psso** = pass slipped stitch over; **rem** = remaining; **rep** = repeat; **RS** = right side; **s** = slip; **st(s)** = stitch(es); **st st** = stocking stitch; **tbl** = through back of loop; **tog** = together; **WS** = wrong side.

BACK

With 3.25mm needles and MC, cast on 106(112:122:134:142:150:156) sts.
Row 1: *K2, P2, rep from * to last 2 sts, K2.
Row 2: P2, *K2, P2, rep from * to end.
Work 11 more rows in K2, P2 rib.
Row 14: P7(10:11:7:7:5:8), P2tog, (P11(11:7:5:4:4:4), P2tog) 7(7:11:17:21:23:23) times, P6(9:10:6:7:5:8). [98(104:110:116:120:126:132) sts.]
Change to 4mm needles and proceed as follows:
Row 1: K.
Row 2: P.
Working in st st, cont until back measures 40(41:42:43:44:45:46)cm, ending with a WS row.

Shape raglan

Cast off 4(5:5:6:7:8:8) sts at beg of next 2 rows. [90(94:100:104:106:110:116) sts.]

Row 1: K1, s1, K1, psso, K to last 3 sts, K2tog, K1. [88(92:98:102:104:108:114) sts.]

Row 2: P1, P2tog, P to last 3 sts, P2tog tbl, P1. [86(90:96:100:102:106:112) sts.]

Rows 1 and 2 set raglan shapings.

Work 0(0:4:4:4:6:8) rows, dec 1 st as before at each end of every row. [86(90:88:92:94:94:96) sts.]

**Proceed as follows:

Row 1: K1, s1, K1, psso, K to last 3 sts, K2tog, K1. [84(88:86:90:92:92:94) sts.]

Row 2: P.

Rows 1 and 2 set raglan shapings.

Work 46(48:48:50:52:52:54) rows, dec 1 st as before at each end of next and every foll alt row. [38(40:40:42:42:42:44) sts.]

Leave rem 38(40:40:42:42:42:44) sts on a stitch holder.

PLACEMENT OF CHART

Follow patt for front as below until work measures 15(17:19:21:23:24:26)cm, ending with a WS row.

Next row: K24(27:30:33:35:38:41) sts in MC, pm, K across 50 sts of 1st row of chart, pm, K across rem of row in MC. This row shows placement of chart.

Complete 86 rows of chart.

At the same time: Cont working front patt shapings.

FRONT

Work as given for Back to **.

Work 34(36:34:36:38:38:38) rows, dec 1 st as before at each end of next and every foll alt row. [52(54:54:56:56:56:58) sts.]

Shape neck

Next row: K1, s1, K1, psso, K14, turn, leave rem 35(37:37:39:39:39:41) sts on a stitch holder. Working on these 16 sts only, proceed as follows for all sizes:

Next row: P.

Next row: K1, s1, K1, psso, K to last 2 sts, K2tog. [14 sts.]

Next row: P2tog, P to end. [13 sts.]

Work 4 rows, dec 1 st as before at raglan edge in next and foll 2nd row.

At the same time: Dec 1 st at neck edge in every row. [7 sts.]

Work 4 rows, dec 1 st as before at each end of next and every foll alt row. [3 sts.]

Next row: K1, s1, K1, psso. [2 sts.]

Next row: P2tog. Fasten off. With RS facing, working on rem 35(37:37:39:39:39:41) sts, slip 18(20:20:22:22:22:24) sts onto a stitch holder, rejoin yarn to rem 17 sts and K to last 3 sts, K2tog, K1. [16 sts.]

Next row: P.

Next row: K2tog, K to last 2 sts, K2tog, K1. [14 sts.]

Next row: Purl to last 2 sts, p2tog. [13 sts.] Work 4 rows, dec 1 st at neck edge in every row.

At the same time: Dec 1 st as before at raglan edge in next and every foll 2nd row. [7 sts.]

Work 4 rows, dec 1 st as before at each end of next and every foll alt row. [3 sts.]

Next row: K1, K2tog. [2 sts.]

Next row: P2tog. Fasten off.

SLEEVES (both alike)

With 3.25mm needles and MC, cast on 58(58:60:60:62:62:64) sts. Work 13 rows in K2, P2 rib.

Row 14: P5(5:2:2:3:3:4), P2tog, (P3(3:4:4:4:4:4), P2tog) 9 times, P6(6:2:2:3:3:4). [48(48:50:50:52:52:54) sts.]

Change to 4mm needles and working in st st, inc 1 st at each end of 5th(5th:3rd:3rd:5th:3rd:3rd) and every foll 8th(8th:8th:6th:6th:6th:6th) row to 62(70:70:60:72:86:86) sts. Inc 1 st at each end of every foll 10th(10th:10th:8th:8th:8th:8th) row to 72(74:76:80:84:88:90) sts. Cont without shaping until sleeve measures 46(46:46:46:47:47:48)cm or length required, ending with WS row.

Shape raglan

Cast off 4(5:5:6:7:8:8) sts at beg of next 2 rows. [64(64:66:68:70:72:74) sts.]

Row 1: K1, s1, K1, psso, K to last 3 sts, K2tog, K1. [62(62:64:66:68:70:72) sts.]

Row 2: P.

Rows 1 and 2 set raglan shapings.

Work 8(10:14:14:14:18:18) rows, dec 1 st as before at each end of 3rd and every foll 4th row. [58(58:58:60:62:62:64) sts.]

Work 40(40:38:40:42:40:42) rows, dec 1 st as before at each end of next and every foll alt row. [18(18:20:20:20:22:22) sts.]

Leave rem 18(18:20:20:20:22:22) sts on a stitch holder.

NECKBAND

Join raglan seams leaving left back raglan open. With RS facing, using MC and 3.25mm needles, work across 18(18:20:20:20:22:22) sts left on stitch holder at top of left sleeve as follows: K8(8:9:9:9:10:10), K2tog, K8(8:9:9:9:10:10), pick up and knit 15 sts evenly along left side of neck, work across 18(20:20:22:22:22:24) sts left on stitch holder at front of neck as follows: K3(4:4:5:5:5:6), K2tog, K8, K2tog, K3(4:4:5:5:5:6), pick up and knit 15 sts evenly along right side of neck, work across 18(18:20:20:20:22:22) sts left on stitch holder at top of right sleeve as follows: K8 (8:9:9:9:10:10), K2tog, K8(8:9:9:9:10:10), and work across 38(40:40:42:42:42:44) sts left on stitch holder at back of neck as follows: K6(7:7:8:8:8:9), K2tog, (K6, K2tog) 3 times, K6(7:7:8:8:8:9). [114(118:122:126:126:130:134) sts.]

Starting with 2nd row of K2, P2 rib, work 9 rows.

Cast off in rib.

TO MAKE UP

Join left back raglan and neckband seams. Join side and sleeve seams. Weave in all ends. Pin out garment to the measurements given. Cover with damp cloths and leave until dry. See ball band for washing and further care instructions.

- **MC** Red
- **A** White
- **B** Black
- **C** Pale pink

Rudolph

If one thing really kicked off the jumper revival it was the fun festive knit. From Bridget Jones's Mr Darcy to Christmas Jumper Day in aid of Save the Children, a novelty nativity knit is fast becoming a Great British tradition. Here we have Welsh wonder and The One Show *presenter Alex Jones, who is as beautiful as she is brilliant, showing us how it is done in this ravishing reindeer design. P.S. Did you know that Rudolph the Red-Nosed Reindeer first appeared in 1939? He was originally going to be called Rollo or Reginald before writer Robert L. May plumped for Rudolph.*

MEASUREMENTS

To fit chest/bust: 81(86:91:97:102:107:112)cm
Length: 68(69:70:71:72:73:74)cm
Sleeve length: 50cm
Figures in brackets refer to the larger sizes.
Where only one figure is given this refers to all sizes.

MATERIALS

7(8:8:9:9:10:10) x 50g balls of 4-ply yarn in main shade – dark green (MC)
1 x 50g ball of 4-ply yarn in each of contrast shades – dark brown (A) and light camel (B)
Small amounts of 4-ply yarn in contrast shades – red (C), black (D) and white (E)
1 pair each of 2.75mm and 3.25mm knitting needles
2 stitch holders
2 stitch markers
The quantities of yarn given are based on average requirements and are therefore approximate.

TENSION

28 stitches and 36 rows to 10cm square over st st on 3.25mm needles (or size needed to obtain given tension).

ABBREVIATIONS

alt = alternate; **beg** = beginning; **cont** = continue; **dec** = decrease; **foll** = following; **inc** = increase; **K** = knit; **K2tog** = knit 2 together; **P** = purl; **P2tog** = purl 2 together; **patt** = pattern; **pm** = place marker; **psso** = pass slipped stitch over; **rem** = remaining; **rep** = repeat; **RS** = right side; **s** = slip; **st(s)** = stitch(es); **st st** = stocking stitch; **tbl** = through back of loop; **tog** = together; **WS** = wrong side.

BACK

With 2.75mm needles and MC, cast on 123(129:135:147:153:159:165) sts.
Row 1 (RS): *K2, P1, rep from * to end.
Row 2: *K1, P2, rep from * to end.
Work 20 more rows in K2, P1 rib.
Change to 3.25mm needles and proceed as follows:
Row 1: K.
Row 2: P.
Working in st st, cont until back measures 38(39:40:41:42:43:44)cm, ending with a WS row.

Shape armholes

Row 1: K1, s1, K1, psso, K to last 3 sts, K2tog, K1. [121(127:133:145:151:157:163) sts.]
Row 2: P1, P2tog, P to last 3 sts, P2tog tbl, P1. [119(125:131:143:149:155:161) sts.]
Rows 1 and 2 set decreases for armholes.

Work 6 rows, dec 1 st as before at each end of every row. [107(113:119:131:137:143:149) sts.]
** Cont in st st without shaping until armhole measures 24cm, ending with WS row.

Shape shoulders

Cast off 6(7:7:8:9:9:10) sts at beg of next 8 rows, then cast off 5(4:6:7:6:8:7) sts at beg of next 2 rows. [49(49:51:53:53:55:55) sts.] Leave rem 49(49:51:53:53:55:55) sts on a stitch holder.

PLACEMENT OF CHART

Follow patt for front as below until work measures 15(16:17:18:19:20:21)cm, ending with a WS row.
Next row: K29(32:35:41:44:47:50) sts in MC, pm, K across 65 sts of 1st row of chart, pm, K across rem of row in MC. This row shows placement of chart. Complete 110 rows of chart.
At the same time: Cont working front patt shapings.

FRONT

Work as given for Back to **. Cont in st st without shaping until armhole measures 16cm ending with WS row.

Shape neck

Next row: K39(42:44:49:52:54:57), K2tog, turn, leave rem 66(69:73:80:83:87:90) sts on a stitch holder. Working on these 40(43:45:50:53:55:58) sts only, proceed as follows:
Next row: P2tog, P to end. [39(42:44:49:52:54:57) sts.]
Work 10 rows, dec 1 st as before at neck edge in every row. [29(32:34:39:42:44:47) sts.]
Cont straight until front measures the same as back to beg of shoulder shaping, ending with WS row.
Cast off 6(6:7:8:8:9:9) sts at beg of next and foll 3 alt rows. [5(8:6:7:10:8:11) sts.]
Work 1 row. Cast off rem 5(8:6:7:10:8:11) sts. With RS facing, working on rem 66(69:73:80:83:87:90) sts, slip 25(25:27:28:30:31:31) sts onto a stitch holder, rejoin yarn to rem 41(44:46:51:54:56:59) sts, K2tog, K to end of row. [40(43:45:50:53:55:58) sts.]
Next row: P to last 2 sts, P2tog tbl. [39(42:44:49:52:54:57) sts.]
Work 10 rows, dec 1 st as before at neck edge in every row. [29(32:34:39:42:44:47) sts.]
Cont straight until front measures the same as back to beg of shoulder shaping ending with RS row.
Cast off 6(6:7:8:8:9:9) sts at beg of next and foll 3 alt rows. [5(8:6:7:10:8:11) sts.]
Work 1 row. Cast off rem 5(8:6:7:10:8:11) sts.

SLEEVES (both alike)

With 2.75mm needles and MC, cast on 69 sts, work 22 rows in K2, P1 rib. Change to 3.25mm needles and working in st st, inc 1 st at each end of 6th and every foll 4th row to 133 sts.
Cont without shaping until sleeve measures 48cm, or length required, ending with a WS row.

Shape armholes

Row 1: K1, s1, K1, psso, K to last 3 sts, K2tog, K1. [131 sts.]
Row 2: P1, P2tog, P to last 2 sts, P2tog tbl, P1. [129 sts.]
Rows 1 and 2 set armhole shapings. Work 6 rows, dec 1 st as before at each end every row. [117 sts.]
Cast off.

NECKBAND

Join left shoulder seam. With RS facing, using MC and 2.75mm needles, work across 49(49:51:53:53:55:55) sts left on stitch holder at back of neck, pick up and knit 23(25:24:24:24:25:25) sts evenly along left side of

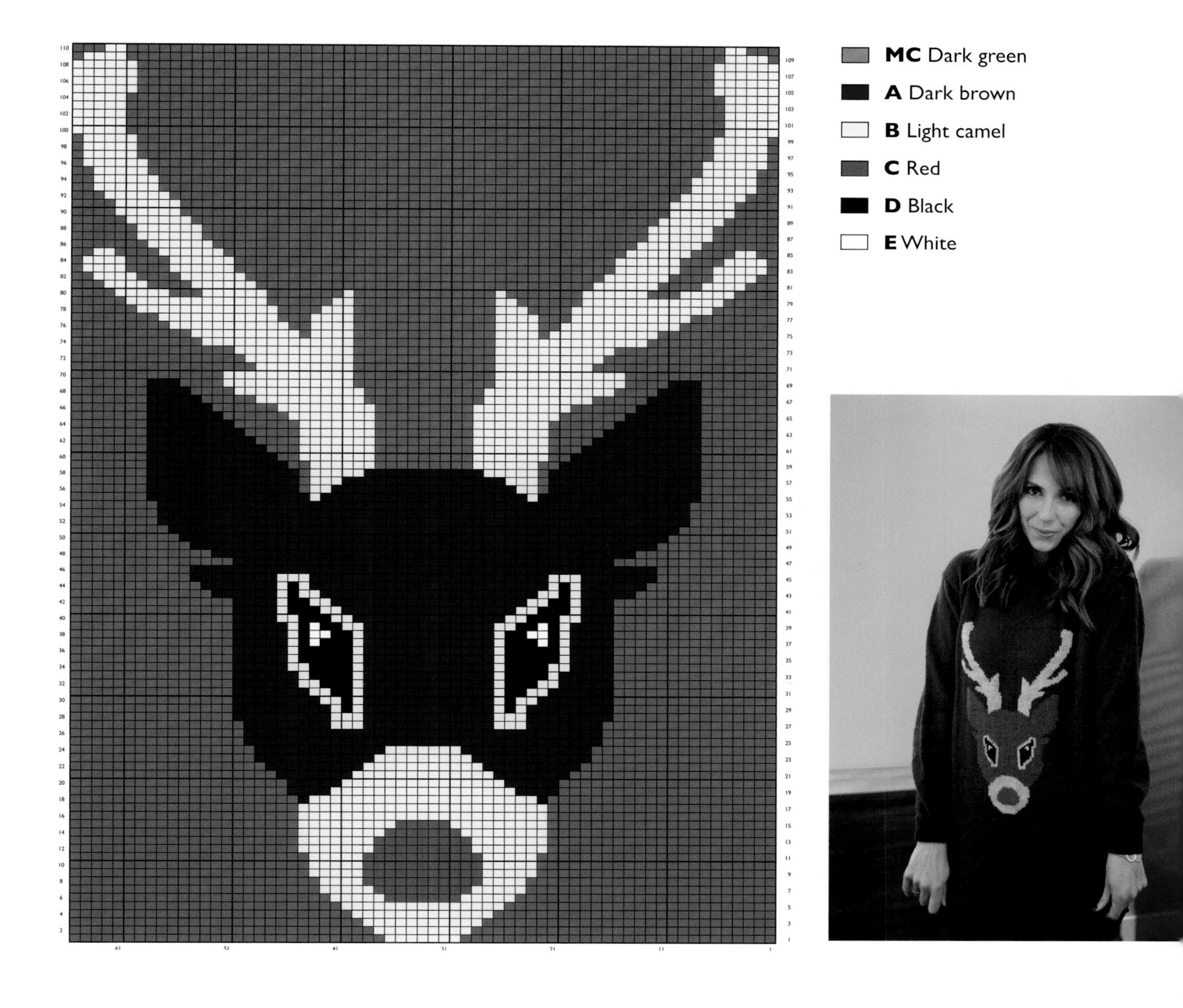

neck, work across 25(25:27:29:29:31:31) sts left on stitch holder at front of neck, pick up and knit 23(24:24:23:23:24:24) sts evenly along right side of neck. [120(123:126:129:129:135:135) sts.]
Starting with 2nd row of K2, P1 rib, work 12 rows. Cast off in rib.

TO MAKE UP

Join right shoulder and neckband seams. Sew in sleeves. Join side and sleeve seams. Weave in all ends. Pin out garment to the measurements given. Cover with damp cloths and leave until dry. See ball band for washing and further care instructions.

Knitting techniques

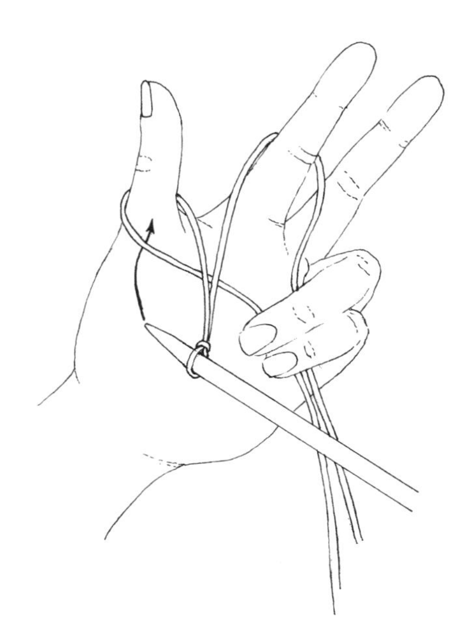

CASTING ON

There are many different ways to cast on, but below are two of the easiest and most commonly used methods. Try not to cast on the yarn too tightly, as it will be difficult to knit the first row.

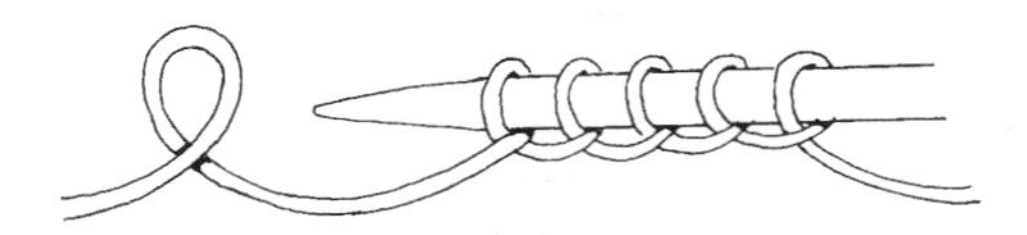

BACKWARD-LOOP CAST-ON METHOD

The easiest cast-on method, best for beginners. Place your left index finger under the yarn and wind it around your finger once, then insert the tip of the needle into the loop in the direction of the end of your finger. Remove your finger and pull the yarn tight. Repeat until you have cast on the desired number of stitches.

THUMB CAST-ON METHOD

This method gives a more elastic edge to the knitting and uses just one needle.

1 Unwind a strand of yarn a little more than three times the length you need for your first row. You may want to add a little extra if you are using a wider needle. Wind the yarn twice around the thumb of your left hand.

2 Put the right-hand needle through the loop and pull through to form a slip knot.

3 Holding the needle in your right hand, loop the loose strand of yarn around your left thumb anticlockwise and the other strand of yarn around your left index finger, as shown.

4 Slide the needle under the front of the loop around your thumb, then through the back of the loop around your index finger, then remove your thumb so the loop drops onto the needle and pull tight.

5 Continue in this way until you have cast on the desired number of stitches.

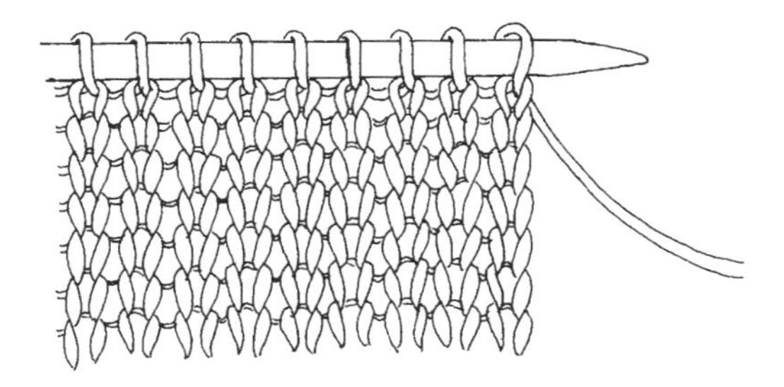

STOCKING STITCH

The jumpers in this book area knitted in stocking stitch, which has a right and wrong side. The stitch is formed by alternate rows of knitting and purling.

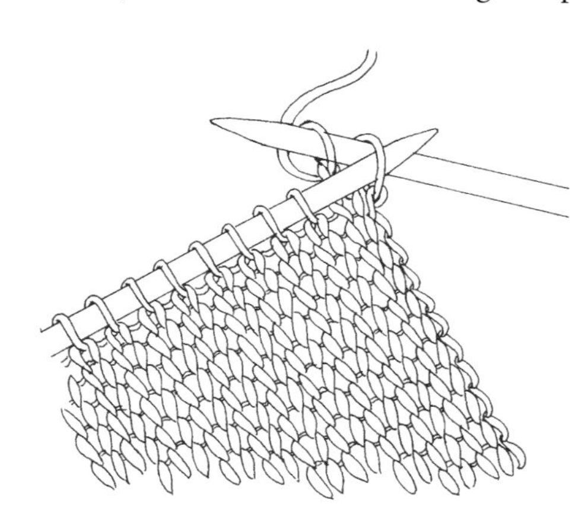

CASTING OFF

Casting off secures the last row of stitches so they don't unravel. If a pattern doesn't tell you which side to cast off, use the right side of the work.

1 Knit the first two stitches of the row.

2 With the yarn at the back of the work, insert the left needle into the last stitch you knitted. Bring this stitch over the second stitch and off the end of your right needle, so there is one stitch left on your right needle, then knit a stitch on your left needle.

3 Repeat step 2 until your left needle is empty and only one stitch remains on your right needle. Break the yarn, pull the end through the last stitch, then pull tight.

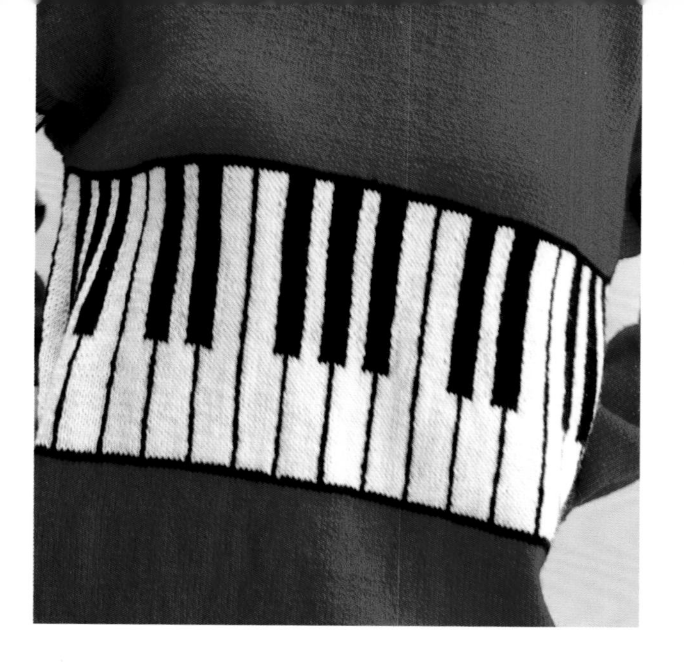

INTARSIA (COLOUR WORK)

This is a popular method of knitting when working with motifs and all the jumpers in this book have a charted motif, making them easier to follow. Each square on the chart represents a stitch and each horizontal line of squares represents a row of stitches. Charts are usually read from bottom to top and right to left, so the first stitch of a chart is at the bottom right-hand corner. They are also usually worked in stocking stitch, with the odd-numbered rows being knit and the even-numbered rows being purl.

Start by winding each coloured yarn you are using around bobbins to prevent the strands from becoming tangled. These can hang at the back of the project while you knit. Work the first stitch by inserting the right needle into the stitch and passing the old yarn over the new yarn to introduce the new colour. Always pass the old yarn over the new yarn and you won't go wrong – do this every time you introduce a new yarn colour. On the back of the work the yarns will loop around each other along the edges of the motif, which will avoid holes from forming on the right side of the work. Ensure that you weave in the tails at the back of the work when you have finished. Uneven stitches can be fixed by steaming lightly with an iron and damp cloth.

The book is based on the creative genius of our favourite knitwear designers: George Hostler, Linda O'Brien, and Sarah Kim.

Some of the jumpers were originally knitted by their designers. Others have been specially knitted for us and we extend our warm thanks to: Karen Hatton, Lynne McFarlane, Pam Wake, Susan Hyams, Helen Scott, Sally Strawberry, Denise Beckerleg, Lesley Hutchinson, Jean Luff, Karen Stow, Sue McBride, Claire Sounes, Roberta Couchman, Vanessa Hubbard, Rose Lee, Tatiana Browne, Charlotte Mace, Victoria Berry, Verna Acres and Sarah Kim.

The patterns have been checked by Victoria Berry and Marilyn Wilson.

Special thanks to our photographer Ingrid Rassmussen and to Francis Loney who took the photographs of the jumpers dating from the 1980s.

Special thanks, too, to the team at Kyle Books: Kyle Cathie, Judith Hannam, Claire Rogers, Clare Sayer, Julia Barder and Hannah Todd.

Gyles and gorgeous George, knitwear designer extraordinaire, posing in a couple of George's creations for Wit Knits in 1986.

Finally, our particular thanks to our amazing models:

Vassos Alexander
Jane Asher
Matt Baker
Hugh Bonneville
Aphra Brandreth
Kosha Engler
Mark Evans
Peter Ginn
Martha Harlan
James Hattsmith
Captain Martin Hewitt
Alex Jones
Shappi Khorsandi
Joanna Lumley
Emma McQuiston
Justine Roberts
Kandy Rohmann
Jake Spark

Here is Linda, as stylish, unique and glamourous as her designs, modelling for us with Gyles in 1987.